Communities in Action

COMMUNITIES
IN ACTION 34

Pattern and Process

by
SEVERYN T. BRUYN
Illinois College

Foreword by
IRWIN T. SANDERS
Boston University

 COLLEGE AND UNIVERSITY PRESS
New Haven, Connecticut

MANUFACTURED IN THE UNITED STATES OF AMERICA BY
UNITED PRINTING SERVICES, INC.
NEW HAVEN, CONN.

TO MY WIFE

FOREWORD

Anyone who has followed the community development field for many years cannot help being impressed with its increasing maturity. In the early 1940's when I was preparing a community organization handbook in the U.S. Department of Agriculture, the chief emphasis was upon the "how to do it" features. We felt at that time that the behavioral sciences could provide us with insights so sufficient that we could prescribe in a general sort of way how successful programs could be carried out. Now, twenty years later, we are not so naive. We know that one does not merely "apply" social science precepts to community development; instead, one uses social science concepts to try to understand the process through which community improvements may be achieved. Community betterment programs, we now know, are much more likely to succeed if those responsible for them can see the process unfolding and adjust to changing circumstances with the over-all process in view. Not all helpful participants need to be intimately knowledgeable about the stages through which a program goes, but those directing the program certainly should be.

At best, process is a vague term. One cannot see, feel, or bump into a process; one only infers from human behavior that it is occurring. Yet, a major contribution that Professor Bruyn has made in this very valuable book is the detailed way he has traced various processes by the use of concrete case studies, while at the same time developing a reasonable, practical model for the analysis of these processes. This work represents a blending of sound social science with the requirements of social action. In being scientific, it tests and moves beyond common-sense observation to the treatment of numerous factors, some of which really lie beneath the surface of community life, usually unperceived until they rear their ugly heads in dramatic fashion. A good model helps to identify in advance what these variables may be so that they can be taken into account before it is too late.

But a model does more than this. It provides a basis, always tentative, for comparing data drawn from one case with data drawn from another case. It is tentative, for it is always in need of further refinement as new data, new insights are revealed and found to be adequately covered by the model. Yet, the model never represents completely any particular case. If it should become so specific it would lose its comparative uses. On the other hand, if it is very abstract its relevance for action purposes becomes more obscure.

Perhaps citizens who are concerned with the improvement of their own community, and only with that, have less need for a model than the consultant who is working with two, three, or twenty communities. But a model can serve the local citizenry too. Each person tends to see the community from his own vantage point, from his own little keyhole. A model can broaden his vision by calling to his attention items which would not otherwise be taken into account. For one thing, he learns that the community and the community development process is more complex than at first assumed. Here truly lies the way of wisdom, since many community efforts fail because those in charge take too few variables into account; their view is oversimplified.

To the social scientist, a model such as the one Professor Bruyn has drawn up serves as a way of making knowledge about community processes cumulative. Each new case can add its contribution since it either reaffirms or calls into question the propositions derived from the model. Case studies which are unrelated to each other make interesting reading, but they do not by themselves enrich the understanding of what really happens in community development programs until they are viewed in keeping with some conceptual scheme and its derivative propositions—which we call a model.

Finally, what has been demonstrated here is that action itself follows some kind of sequence which can be ordered into a model; since this is true, it makes little sense for the action-oriented person to deride the person who is trying to understand the process. By the same token, the model builder should realize his dependence upon those engaged in action for the concrete data, carefully observed and recorded, which help him form and continually test the model. Community development as a national and even as a world-wide movement will only come into its own as there is a skilful blending of theory and action, of program formulation and testing, and a search by all concerned for the generic traits of the community development process.

IRWIN T. SANDERS

Boston University

ACKNOWLEDGMENTS

Portions of this study were originally part of a doctoral dissertation presented at the University of Illinois in Urbana. I am indebted to the following people for their assistance in making the present work possible: to Professor Robert W. Janes of the University of Illinois for his suggestions and guidance in designing the original study; to Professor Richard W. Poston of the University of Southern Illinois for so generously providing the author with his personal knowledge of consulting activities and making department files available for research; to former President H. Gary Hudson of Illinois College and Professor Malcolm F. Stewart who together created the basis for and personally supported the college-community program; to the consultants and many citizens who so kindly offered their assistance in reconstructing events in the programs; to Professor Richard E. Palmer of MacMurray College for critically reading sections of the final manuscript. The responsibility for any errors which may be found in the present study are assumed entirely by the author.

S.T.B.

TABLE OF CONTENTS

TABLE OF CONTENTS

INTRODUCTION

SINCE WORLD WAR II an increasing consciousness of the large forces at work in society has become evident. On the one hand there is a growing sense of isolation and alienation in modern society, and on the other hand a moving but sometimes deviant search for community. This escape from isolation and search for community has taken several directions.

One direction is illustrated in the widely read studies of *The Organization Man* and *The Lonely Crowd*.[1] In modern society man has had to adjust to many large-scale associations and to a high degree of social mobility. The security and sense of identity he formerly found in the family, the neighborhood, the local community, the church, have gradually disappeared. In place of these primary institutions he has become involved in the massive forces of urbanization, industrialization, and bureaucracy. In his efforts to recover a sense of community he has sought togetherness in his immediate group. He looks to those about him for the answers to basic questions of life. He can ignore tradition; he finds it difficult to stand on his own principles; he looks to the group for social approval. But this search has been superficial and has resulted only in deepening man's feeling of isolation.

A second direction which the search has taken is illustrated in Orwell's *1984*, Fromm's *Escape From Freedom*, and Huxley's *Brave New World*[2] where the state becomes the community. It, too, represents a response to large-scale society; however, in this case the community is identified in only one association, the political. The rise of totalitarianism, whether it be in Europe, Asia, Africa, or even America, cannot properly be understood apart from this deep longing for community. In many of the developing countries this kind of search has now taken the form of passionate movements for nationalism and economic growth.

For the Western intellectual today, however, there is an exhaustion of Utopia, as Daniel Bell has phrased it, an "end to ideology." The passion which entered sensibly into the reform movements of the nineteenth century is no longer with him; the old ideologies have served their time and have lost their power. He finds no countermovement, only static transition. It is static because the society is without clear direction and national purpose; yet the forces are still at work. In spite of the awesome ideological struggle between the East and the West—so repeatedly referred to and daily dramatized—he is confronted on all sides by the same story of large-scale organization of society. For all the apparent differences between the "free" and the "collective" societies, he still perceives a growing similarity between the Western position as it approaches centralization and the Eastern as it approaches industrialization and all its consequences.

The giant nation-states inevitably have become attractive models to those developing countries which are trying to pull themselves into the twentieth century. Before these developing countries stand images of power, but power manifest in sprawling cities and slums, standardized assembly lines, centralized authorities, mass communications, and mass man. As the large nations influence the social and economic development of the smaller ones, the consequences to the individual and his own deviant search for community are profound. The question arises whether this pattern of development is an inevitable and unavoidable one. Do viable alternatives exist to encourage or allow other forces to exert their transforming influence on the character of modern society?

There is still a third manifestation of the search for community in Western society. This movement is basically social rather than individual or political.[3] It began early in the nineteenth century in Europe and America, at a time when the forces of modern society were just beginning to take shape. Since its inception it has taken many forms; today it comprehends a tradition of activity in social work, academic studies, university extension programs, and internationally sponsored community development programs.

In the scope of this movement is a renewed interest on the part of citizens in communities across the nation to take action to solve their problems locally. Included also is the growing interest, on the part of institutions of higher education, in the field of community organization and development. Increasingly, concerned communities call upon the university to furnish knowledge about community development and even to assist in taking action. In fulfilling these functions the university seeks to accumulate empirical knowledge of the ways in which communities operate, by carefully observing what happens when communities attempt to implement these suggestions. Furnishing a community consultant is one way in which the university assists—and at the same time observes—community development. The present study is a report on the different ways in which four communities sought to improve local conditions when a small college and university expressed an interest in working with them.

DESIGN OF STUDY

The study focuses on what happened in four Illinois communities when significant portions of the local population were aroused to take action on their mutual problems. The particular method which they used for taking action is an important part of the study. There are two methods, described in the literature on community action, which were employed in the cases under study. The two approaches have many of the same qualities and are difficult to distinguish except by way of the emphasis given to certain phases of the community action process.

One method has developed within the field of social work and has frequently employed the phrase "community organization" to describe the way citizens and professionals can work to solve local problems. An important way people organize to treat their problems is through a *community council*. In this study the agency which emphasized this approach was Illinois College, a small liberal arts institution in west-central Illinois. Two communities were selected which had organized community councils to treat their local problems. These were Jacksonville and Chapin.

Another method described in this study has more frequently employed the terms "community development."[4] A significant example of this type of approach was initiated at the University of Montana.[5] The experiments begun there were extended to the University of Washington and then to Southern Illinois University where a department of community development was established. An important means by which people organize for action in this approach is through a *self-study*. The two other cases studied herein were selected from a series of programs initiated by southern Illinois townspeople in cooperation with staff members from the University at Carbondale. The communities selected for study are Eldorado and Cobden.

PURPOSE OF STUDY

It is not the purpose of this study to evaluate the over-all effectiveness of these two approaches to community action nor to judge the value of the educational programs at the two institutions. To achieve the former purpose would require a cross-country survey. To achieve the latter purpose would be virtually impossible since the two programs were organized in different grounds, the college (on a small scale) emphasizing student education, the university (on a larger scale) emphasizing adult education. The over-all educational activities and aims of these institutional programs are available in the literature distributed by each institution. The focus of this study is upon the communities themselves, and the way in which they approached their problems with varying degrees of assistance.

The cases were selected after the action programs had been in operation for at least three years. They were chosen out of an objective interest in the action process and not for public relations purposes. This meant selecting cases which ranged from relative success to relative lack of success, as judged by citizens involved in them. The choice of a program which did not achieve what was expected of it might have been made in either approach, the self-study or the council approach. As it was, the university's self-study approach had witnessed un-completed programs similar to the college experience represented in the Jacksonville study.[6] Although the council approach had no case which paralleled the intensity and excitement of the Eldorado story, it had its own measurable achievements. Inter-estingly enough Eldorado was found to have failed, at certain points, to achieve its aims, and the uncompleted program (Jacksonville) was found to have achieved something of its purposes.[7] Chapin and Cobden ranged between these extremes.

The purpose of this study is to examine the action process in depth: to analyze the parts of each process which appeared to block effectiveness and the parts which appeared to advance the purposes set down in the community programs. Without explicit reference to functional theory the study is concerned with the latent, the manifest, the functional, and the dysfunctional elements in these programs.[8]

The study examines two models of community action and their effects on the social structures in each community. It examines the kind of roles taken by consultants who ranged from a minimum to a maximum degree of personal involvement. It considers one community in detail in order to comprehend how radical change took place from the point of view of the people involved. It explains this change from a scientific point of view and reviews some of the problems involved in making the transition from the cultural world of the active participant to the cultural world of the scientist as each seeks to explain the action process. The underlying assumption of this study is that it is important to understand both worlds in the field of community development.

INSTITUTIONAL SETTINGS

These models were transmitted through institutions of higher education to local communities by way of special community programs organized in each institution. The agency and the structure of its community program is an important factor to take into consideration in understanding the general outcome of action programs.

West-central Illinois

West-central Illinois is largely agricultural, with small to middle-sized towns and cities containing diversified business and industry. In the heart of the region is a small liberal arts college, Illinois College, founded in 1829.

In 1950, in cooperation with the state department of public welfare, the college established a program in community organization whose purpose was (1) to cooperate with communities as they seek to develop their resources and meet their needs through voluntary group action, and (2) to provide a means through which students may study the community while participating in its efforts to deal with its own problems.

A staff of two to three persons taught classes in various years and served as part-time consultants to communities seeking to improve local conditions. In different ways, students became an important part of the process of community action taking place in the region. Students studied the community from an academic point of view while at the same time participating in community programs with citizens. A description of the two-semester course in which a number of students participated each year is an important subject in itself, but cannot be treated here. It should be said, however, that the education of students was of primary concern to the college and basic to the establishment of the program.

The community council approach was emphasized by the college staff as an important way for citizens to treat their general community problems. But it represents only one of many ways in which the college program related to communities in its region. There were special projects of staff members such as community surveys, leadership training programs, radio programs, community conferences, newsletters, etc. These activities all combined in an educational program designed to relate the academic interests of the college with the reality of community life and its needs in modern society.

Southern Illinois

The region in which the other two case studies are located is not so rich in agriculture. In the past, Southern Illinois had depended heavily upon the coal mining industry. As the coal mines were closed down the whole region suffered a severe economic crisis.

In 1953, Southern Illinois University established a department of community development to bring into operation community programs which would constructively relate to the needs of the region. The director stated what he considered to be the initial problems of the new program.[9]

> The primary problems of the Department during the three and one-half years since its establishment have been to devise a practical set of techniques and procedures for actual operating purposes, to evolve an effective operating policy, to build a staff organization through which the purposes of the program can be achieved within the particular social and economic context of southern Illinois, and to properly establish itself as an existing entity within the region.

The community programs which have developed through the department are much more diversified than the cases selected would indicate, and they should not be taken as being necessarily typical. The department considers each community unique in itself, and its needs must in large measure determine which methods should be followed.

The Method

Research was conducted in each community through interviews with local citizens and a study of local documents. Methods of investigation are described in more detail before the presentation of each research problem. Six research problems were posed in making the investigation. They are as follows:

I. IDEAL MODELS—What were the ideal models which each action program put into practice?

II. ACTION STORIES—(a) How did action take place in each community? (b) What roles did the consultants take in each community?

III. INFLUENCE—What kinds of influence or effects were produced in the communities?

IV. DETERMINANTS—What were the determinants of the influence created in the communities?

V. PROBLEMS AND POSSIBILITIES—(a) Why did the ideal models not work entirely as expected? (b) What conditions must be created to reach the objectives?

VI. COMMUNITY DEVELOPMENT PROCESS—(a) How does a community undergo *radical social change*, guided by an outside agency? (b) How can this process be analyzed?

NOTES

1. William H. Whyte, Jr., *The Organization Man* (New York: Simon and Schuster, 1956); David Reisman, in collaboration with Reuel Denny and Nathan Glazer, *The Lonely Crowd* (New Haven: Yale University Press, 1950).

2. George Orwell, *Nineteen Eighty Four* (New York: Harcourt, Brace & Co., 1949); Erich Fromm, *Escape From Freedom* (New York: Rinehart & Co., 1941); Aldous Huxley, *Brave New World and Brave New World Revisited* (New York: Harper & Brothers, 1960).

3. A brief description of the movement is found in the Appendix.

4. The terms "community organization" and "community development" are used here because they were expressed by staff members of each respective institution to describe their approach. A more generalized meaning may be found in the Appendix.

5. Baker Brownell, *The Human Community* (New York: Harper & Brothers, 1950); Richard Poston, *Small Town Renaissance* (New York: Harper & Brothers, 1950).

6. An analysis of a self-study program in southern Illinois which failed to complete its schedule may be found in Samuel W. Byuarm, "Community Action: A Case Study in Racial Cleavage" (unpublished Ph.D. dissertation, University of Illinois, 1962).

7. Further research may prove Jacksonville to be the most typical of the four cases studied. In Michigan, the average life of 59 per cent of 120 councils in existence between 1939 and 1946 was two years. See Appendix page 178.

8. R. K. Merton, *Social Theory and Social Structure* (Glencoe, Illinois: The Free Press, 1949).

9. Richard Poston, "Foreword," *A Report on the Plans and Operations of the Department of Community Development* (Carbondale, Illinois: Southern Illinois University, 1957), p. iii.

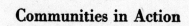

Communities in Action

Communities in Action

CHAPTER 1

IDEAL MODELS

*What were the ideal models which each action
program put into practice?*

THE COMMUNITY COUNCIL APPROACH

TO OBTAIN IDEAL DESCRIPTIONS of the community
council approach, it was necessary to survey the agencies
which provide published information about the council.
Agencies which published such information were found among
the following: (1) national welfare associations (e.g., Community
Chests and Councils of America, American Association for Adult
Education, National Planning Association); (2) state adult
education associations and state boards of community organization and delinquency prevention; (3) metropolitan social planning councils; (4) private social work agencies; (5) university
extension services and academic departments wherein texts and
pamphlets are written on community organization. The names
of council organizations which are suggested by the publications
emanating from these varied sources are equally as varied and
include such terms as the following: community council, district
council, social planning council, council of social agencies,
welfare federation, welfare council, etc. In our case communities,
the term "community council" was used. Some of the published
sources which are used to describe the ideal model in this
section were used as a guide by the consultants in organizing
the council in the west-central Illinois communities under
study. A documentation of the models used in community
action programs follows.

Ideology

Philosophy

A policy statement on community planning and social welfare was made by the Community Chests and Councils which it claimed was an effort to bring together different emphases into one clear presentation. The points listed under the philosophy underlying this approach are as follows:[1]

1. Each individual has a basic responsibility to meet his own needs to the extent of his ability. But people are interdependent; the welfare of each affects the welfare of all. It is natural and necessary that people form organizations to work for their mutual benefit.

2. The need for community planning for social welfare stems from the wants and desires of all people; and all interests and elements of the population have a right and a responsibility to participate in it.

3. Community planning for social welfare is concerned with the welfare of the community and the total life of the individual, taking account of his physical, mental, emotional and spiritual needs.

4. Fundamental to community planning is acceptance of change and development of social services to keep pace with changes in social conditions, in knowledge of social problems, and in concepts of human well-being.

5. While agencies and organizations in the American system are self-determining and autonomous they are mutually inter-related. They come together in a joint cooperative effort in community planning. Community planning, then, is a democratic process in which agencies and organizations, as well as individuals, participate through representatives of their own choosing.

By the term "social welfare" is meant "the well-being of people in the broad sense, encompassing health, social adjustment, recreation, and environmental conditions," whether under governmental auspices or not.

Objectives

The Michigan Council on Adult Education lists the following "specific purposes":[2]

1. To provide an agency through which community groups and individual citizens can become articulate and achieve cooperation.

2. To provide an agency through which all community groups can coordinate their activities for the common good.

3. To carry on long term planning, discover problems, and make recommendations for consideration by the proper authorities.

4. To promote the achievement of community-wide projects, too large or too difficult for any single group to undertake.

5. To stimulate member organizations to a continuous self-evaluation and improvement of their activities.

Functions

The functions of a community council are understood to be the ways in which the action program or its association actually operates within the community context. The functions which are deemed part of the community council are:[3]

A FEDERATION of all community service, civic, and social welfare organizations whose purpose is to develop progressive methods and coordinate efforts in all fields of human welfare, develop mutual understanding and effective working relations.

A MEDIUM through which the collective will of business, education, labor, industrial recreation, health, and social agencies is ascertained and expressed. . . .

A CLEARING HOUSE for all services and agencies engaged in community welfare, providing liaison service and relationships with all appropriating bodies or welfare services, public and private, and providing for new services.

A COOPERATIVE PLANNING BODY that brings together the forces and agencies of the community. . . .

AN ADMINISTRATIVE BODY for such common services as Research, Information, Training of Volunteers, Social Service Exchange, Volunteer Bureau, etc.

The function of the community council for all its member organizations is clearly not an administrative one in the sense that it dictates what projects each organization should undertake; it exists rather as a service for each, a means by which each may voluntarily work together. The over-all function of the action program is to contribute to the general welfare of the community.

Mechanics

Initiation and Organization

The steps to initiate and organize a community council are explicitly stated in dozens of pamphlets on the subject. A recent publication contains the following:[4]

1. Form a small steering committee of interested people, making sure to include a cross-section of religious, racial, economic, and social interests.

2. From the experience of this group, make a list of possible projects which a council might tackle.

3. List the organizations which are potential members of a council.

4. Assign steering committee members to meet with organization representatives to discuss the advantages of a council and draw out the problems which they would like to see discussed.

5. When enough interest seems to have been developed, call a community-wide meeting to which organizations, clubs, agencies, and other groups are asked to send representatives to hear about the nature, purpose, and probable program of a council.

6. Follow the meeting with visits to the meetings of these organizations, and letters asking them to express their opinions about the value of a council and what it should do.

7. Call other community-wide meetings if necessary; it is important at the initial stages of development to take time enough to build a strong foundation.

8. Prepare well for each meeting. . . .

9. Send a report of each meeting to all who attended and to others who were invited but did not come, get subcommittees set up to work on a constitution, on building a file of membership prospects, on a plan for financing the council, and to outline ways in which one or two projects might be handled.

10. The steering committee should meet frequently and regularly during the organizational stages of the council to test the validity of the desire for a council and to plan the next steps. . . .

11. When agreement to organize is reached, temporary officers should be elected to replace the steering committee. Permanent officers will be elected as soon as the constitution has been adopted.

12. The constitution should define the objectives, powers, and functions of the organization as a guide to establishing policy and program. It is well to keep this document simple and clear and not cluttered with administrative details.

Sample constitutions are provided by various agencies. Such samples were followed closely in writing the community council constitutions in Chapin and Jacksonville, our two case studies.

According to every model plan suggested by various agencies, the membership of the community council should be inclusive of all major organizations in the community. More specifically,[5]

> They include service clubs, labor unions, veterans' organizations, women's clubs, fraternal organizations, the Parent-Teacher Association, the Chamber of Commerce, the Council of Churches and other religious groups, the Medical Society, the Dental Society, the Bar Association, the League of Women Voters, and many others.

One pamphlet recognized a common division of labor within the planning programs of a community, but went on to make the "Community Welfare Planning Council" still inclusive of them all.[6]

> The cooperation of three or more planning groups—Chamber of Commerce, Planning Commission, Council of Social Agencies, and special bodies as Labor Unions, Church Federations—is important when the total welfare of the community and the services needed by the community are considered and they should all be a part of an overall Community Welfare Planning Council.

Execution

There are three points which seem to characterize the literature describing the "execution" phase of the model. First, "principles" upon which to take action are more often suggested than the "specific steps" to take in launching the action. Second, certain areas such as health, social welfare, recreation, and housing are emphasized for action, whereas civic improvement, legislation, industrial development are seldom discussed. Third, there is a definite emphasis placed on a paid staff which can stimulate action on community projects.

Some of the paragraph headings of one pamphlet may illustrate the emphasis given as follows: "Paid Staff is Essential to Best Results," "Plan Long Range Financing," "Educate Rather Than Legislate," "Focus on Needs Rather Than Agencies," "Make the Approach Positive," "Creep Before Walking—Walk Before Running," "Keep Planning and Administration Separate."[7]

There are special groups or committees which the literature suggests as valuable to the execution of projects. There should be a board of directors or an exclusive committee (composed of officers and committee chairmen), standing committees (which need to include at least membership, finance, program, and public relations), and project committees (such as health, recreation, child welfare, etc.). The decision as to which problems are to be handled by which committees is left to the discretion of the executive committee.

An example of a specific model which is given in the field of health is abbreviated in outline form below.[8]

  1. *Fact Finding:*
        Obtain available data as to the character and extent of the problem and the resources available to deal with it. . . .

  2. *Planning and Coordinating the Total Program:*
        On the basis of facts which are found, define the problem and the needs, and determine what further steps should be taken to meet the need. . . .

  3. *Stimulating and Influencing Community Action:*
        Organize citizens' support to gain necessary action by officials or voluntary agencies to meet community needs.

  4. *Educating and Interpreting and Informing:*
        Educate the people of the community as to the nature and extent of health problems and what as individuals they can and should do about them. . . .

  5. *Stimulating Increased Participation:*
        Increase citizen participation in the health program either by acceptance of personal responsibility by the individual for himself and his family or by sharing in the work of carrying out a plan.

6. *Suggested Problems:*
   Communicable Disease Control:
   a. Venereal disease control
   b. Tuberculosis control. . . .

Maintenance

The literature indicates clearly that the community council has been organized to last—its purposes, its constitutional organization testify to this fact. However, there is no clear distinction to be found in the literature which demarcates what we have called the "execution phase" and the "maintenance phase." Descriptions of both are made on the level of general principles, and one tends to merge into the other. A typical example of principles and suggestions which have emerged as guides is the following:[9]

1. See that it is the business of someone to follow up on proposals, recommendations, and actions. The successful larger councils employ or have the services of a full-time executive secretary. Everyone's business is apt to become no one's concern.

2. Keep the Council active, studying needs and problems of the community. . . .

3. Refer projects to existing organizations whenever possible and perform only such tasks as cannot be handled by other groups.

4. Meet regularly and have vital matters for consideration at each assembly. Report progress and achievements. Follow up inaction.

5. Elect a chairman with demonstrated ability. . . .

6. Get an efficient secretary with definite time for the job. . . .

7. Call upon and use the services of consultants and specialists in the fields of the community's needs and interests. . . .

8. If the council is large, arrange for effective committees and committee work. . . .

9. Arrange to have finances adequate to meet the plans of the council. Most councils spend very little money but most of them could spend more with a great deal of profit. An executive secretary, postage, telephone, mimeographing, special notices, surveys, and the like are items to consider. Finances must be made to fit projects and plans. Revenues usually come through contributions from private sources, member organizations, community chest, service clubs, or through staging an entertainment

or performance. Funds for special projects are sometimes obtained from the agency for which the services are performed. Money raising projects and schemes should generally be avoided.

The concept which has been most frequently used in literature describing the community council approach is "community organization." The concept most frequently used to describe the next model is "community development."

THE SELF-STUDY APPROACH

The sources of description for this model are not as varied as those for the community council. The approach is still in the process of being formulated and developed through the services of universities and colleges. Nevertheless the main outline of the model has already been described.

Ideology

Philosophy

In his book *The Human Community*, Baker Brownell discusses the dangers of the Western world, with its industrialized cities which have produced human complexities, personal anonymity, and loss of control over man's destiny. He defines the problem in many ways in order to give it meaning and dramatize its significance.[10]

> That problem is the disintegration of the community and its slow extinction in the western world. I am not unaware of the dramatic dangers, atomic and otherwise, that hang over this nation and the modern world. The decline of the human community is nevertheless the primary problem, the germinal problem, so to speak, in all this modern complex of disaster.

Although he writes that he is aware of the common difficulties of the small community—its sordid routines, its narrowness of life—his belief is that this is not beyond recovery and control. The modern city, however, comes under a stronger indictment, and its future, under present conditions, is not as hopeful.[11]

Different from the agglutinative solidarity of urban life is the organic solidarity of the community. The solidarity of the one is massive and undifferentiated so far as the content of each group is concerned. The solidarity of the other is structurally flexible; it is personal, or tends so to be in the communal continuum of face-to-face relationships.

In a mass group the human being tends toward depersonalization. In the authoritarian party, state, or industrial organization he becomes solely a functional instrument. Amid the spectators at a prize fight or a professional presentation of Aida, he tends to become, even to himself, a laugh, a thrill, a clapping of hands, a smart comment, a violent boo. As a personality he is a loser and he compensates by a vast anonymous belonging to the great group. Freedom under these conditions is rarely organic or deeply intentional. Because it is not expressive of a full command of life, it is likely to become, if present at all, little more than shallow erraticism and willfulness.

The organic solidarity of the community, on the other hand, is coherent through personality and freedom. It too is a belonging, but belonging here is personal. It is full belonging in a small group rather than fragmental belonging in a great one. In the mass group part of the spectator's personality is caught up, intensified, and fused. . . .

Community lends itself particularly well to "the continuities of action"; it is the basis of social life and social control. The nature of the community begins and ends with the people who compose it.[12]

What then is the community? My own predispositions lead me to say that men are the measure of their communities, and groups which change in size or quality beyond the measure of a man or beyond his limits of experience are not true communities.

A sense of urgency is imbedded in the writings of Baker Brownell. His writings reflect an emerging ideal of social organization in modern society. This ideal began to take particular form in the Montana Self-Study Program.

Objectives

According to the writings of Richard Poston,[13] the Montana Study began with the primary problem of finding "ways to enrich the quality of living in Montana." Then, "as the planning got under way, the first specific objective was to 'get the University off the campus.'" The second major objective was to "find ways to stabilize the family and the small community." A third and related objective was "to study ways to raise the appreciative and spiritual standard of living of the people of the state and thus keep a larger number of able young people in their home communities."

At the University of Washington, the objectives were defined again with the publication of a set of study guides, but the essential goals and philosophy behind the approach remained the same.[14]

> The development of community life in modern America will reawaken and revitalize democratic processes. It will also provide the social foundation from which America can rise to new heights as a free society, from which the principles of human rights and representative government may regain their vitality, and from which our Republic may renew her moral influence in the world family of nations. But the critical point in the national fabric is the local community. For unless democracy can survive there it cannot survive anywhere.
>
> This is the broad purpose of the community study outlined in this guide. It is a program in community development through which a group of people may sit down together to study life in their own community in order to find out for themselves how to enrich and improve it.

Mechanics

Initiation

Insofar as the model includes the university agency's relationship to the community, a model rule has been established which prohibits the agency from seeking to initiate a particular community program in a particular community. It behooves the community to do the initiating and to contact the university for consultation. A consultant guides the program from that point on. Like the community council, however, the self-study idea has become something which the average citizen can begin himself. The steps for initiation are outlined below:[15]

1. If you already have several people interested in *doing something* about your community problems, organize a temporary

steering committee, made up of as diverse membership as you can get.

2. Keep probing, talking to people, finding out how organizations and "key" figures in the community feel about community development (persons such as the newspaper editor, the mayor, banker, superintendent of schools, real estate owners, union officials, organizational heads, etc.).

3. If there seems to be support for planned development of your community—and no one or few dissenters should have more than their single "vote"—draw a Temporary Executive Committee from the larger Steering Committee and set to work.

4. Create a Publicity or Public Relations Committee to keep everyone informed.

5. You might get volunteers for the Population, Boundary and Mapping Committees and get this fact finding under way early.

6. Begin to prepare for a community-wide meeting, where everyone will help decide whether to launch a program, and where all will have a chance to volunteer for one or more study-action committees. Be sure to have a slate of candidates for various offices to present at this first meeting, but either present two or more candidates for each position, or allow nominations from the floor. You can't strengthen democracy in your town unless you practice it at every turn.

7. Assuming the citizenry favors a CD Program, the new officers can begin setting up the organization and committees, selecting chairmen and discussion teams. The Executive and Advisory Council will need to meet regularly—probably at least once a week for the Committee and once a month for the Council.

Organization[16]

The purposes of the community development program require an organizational structure that will embrace the entire population and make it possible for all existing organizations and agencies in the community to join together in the total effort.

The officers and leaders that are needed for this purpose are as follows:

1. *General Chairman.* To coordinate the entire program.

2. *Vice-Chairman.* To assist the general chairman.

3. *Secretary.* To keep records on the community development program.

4. *Treasurer.* To handle necessary funds.

5. *Chief Recorder.* To assemble the notes from all of the discussion group recorders at each of the town meetings and to prepare report of proceedings for each of these meetings.

6. *Recorders.* To keep notes on the discussions in the various discussion groups at each of the town meetings, and to report back to the general assembly at the close of the discussion period.

7. *Discussion Leaders.* To lead the discussions in each of the discussion groups at the town meetings.

8. *Committee Chairmen.* To chair each of the study-action committees.

9. *Block Unit Leaders.* To arrange for the block unit meetings.

Fact-finding committees are formed to investigate all areas of community life, and to recommend and spearhead whatever specific action projects may be found necessary by the people to accomplish the goals of the program.

In general, these committees are as follows:

1. City Planning Committee
2. Population Committee
    a) Boundary Crew
    b) Mapping Crew
    c) Census Crew
    d) Special Survey Crew (sampling public opinion)
3. Council of Organizations
4. Church Committee
5. Beautification Committee
6. Housing Committee
7. Agriculture Committee
8. Industry Committee
9. Labor Committee
10. Retail Trade and Services Committee
11. Health Committee
12. Recreation Committee

13. Education Committee
14. Library Committee
15. Government Committee
16. Social Welfare Committee
17. History Committee

Each of these committees prepares a detailed report of its findings, conclusions and recommendations for action, and a discussion guide for use in various meetings. The meetings are held throughout the community in order to make it possible for the entire population to participate and to gain a better understanding of specific problems in all areas of community life. These committees are called study-action committees and are responsible for initiating whatever planning or action may be indicated from a study of the facts. They may not be the same in all communities, but are tailored to fit the needs and conditions of the local situation.

Town meetings are fundamental to the program. They are the medium through which the facts are made known to the community. Once each week for a period of three to seven months, an open community meeting is held in the high school auditorium where large numbers of people may attend. At these meetings the study-action committees present their reports and recommendations for action. One or more town meetings are devoted to each committee.

At each of the town meetings after the committee report has been made, all persons at the meeting divide into small discussion groups, or "buzz sessions," to discuss the report and recommendations that have been presented by the committee. Each discussion group meets in a different room of the school building. Each group has its own discussion leader and a person designated as the "recorder" to keep notes on the discussion.

At the close of the discussion period in each town meeting the discussion groups reassemble in the auditorium, and the recorders form a panel to report back on the conclusions and recommendations that were reached in their respective discussion groups.

Since the programs placed in operation in the small "case" communities went into effect, many additional kinds of programs have been added to the university's approach. For example, in order to increase the direct, personal participation of people in large cities, the entire community may be divided into block units small enough to make it possible for all of the families in each unit to meet together in each other's homes. Each block unit may select one action project to improve their neighborhood. The local radio or television station assembles a panel of persons to introduce the discussion for the evening in each block unit. When the panel presentation goes off the air in fifteen or twenty minutes, the block meeting holds a discussion. At the close of the discussion period the radio or television program comes back on the air, and a reporter from each block meeting telephones into the station the conclusions and recommendations for action that have been reached by the people in the meeting. The radio or television station then begins broadcasting these reports so that the people in each block unit meeting throughout the community can hear what has been discussed in the other block unit meetings in the community.

Organizational Functions

The Advisory Council directs the program through the study phase, and following this a "Community Development Association" (CDA) may be established through which the work is to be carried forward on a permanent long-range basis. The Advisory Council and the CDA are similar in composition. Each is composed of elected officers and committee chairmen of action committees. The official transition from study to action generally requires a reorganization of the committee structure and an election of new officers.

In the present description of the self-study program, the "council of organizations" (which is another term for what we have designated community council) may be worked into the initial organizational phase of the program. The place of the council type of organization varies in actual operation among communities in which the self-study model has been placed in operation. For example, in one community there is both a CDA (composed of officers and committee chairmen), and a council of organizations composed of representatives from community organizations. The purpose of the council is to receive ideas and suggestions for projects from CDA and channel them into the appropriate organized groups whose interest or function is designed to take action on them. In another community, CDA is composed of an executive board of elected officers, six to fifteen directors (at large), and one representative from each of nineteen civic organizations. Consultants of the self-study approach state that the organizational structure must be tailored to fit the needs of each particular community.

Each committee has a function within the program as a whole.[17] The function of the study-action committees is to provide the community with knowledge about itself. It is assumed that in the process of fact-finding, the committee will be directed toward taking action, or will motivate others to do so, on specific projects. The function of the Advisory Council and the CDA is to oversee the broader problems and possibilities of the program. It serves as a sustaining force through the ups and downs of committee work. It also functions as a catalyst for action on problems which have not yet been tackled.

Town meetings function to stimulate a feeling of community and to develop common bonds of interest and loyalty. The meeting also functions to give people a chance to stand up and "speak their minds" about what they feel is important to the community. It is also a medium through which public recognition is provided for those citizens who give their time for community development. New leaders have an opportunity to grow into leadership positions through their appearance before town assemblies.

Execution

In executing the self-study phase of the program, the practitioner and citizens have written guides for collecting data. The guides are in books and in mimeographed sheets which are made available to citizens in work committees.

The procedures for taking direct action on specific problems are not so carefully detailed in published form. Concrete illustrations are given verbally by experienced consultants as to how other communities have solved similar problems, but little is published as guides for particular problems such as delinquency, health, etc. Consequently, the model becomes less specific at this point and much is left to the creative powers of the consultant and citizens to work out the problems themselves.

In view of special needs existing in southern Illinois, the university provides technical assistance on such problems as plant location, development of home industry, retail trade, agriculture, city planning, housing, community arts, etc. In these cases specialists are called upon for advice or counsel when action is taken.

Maintenance

The self-study model carries the assumption that a community development association is organized to act in behalf of the whole community and will continue to maintain itself over an indefinite period of years. There are no written guides which deal directly with this phase of the model. This does not mean particular university agencies have not been taking steps to deal with it; it does mean that problems of maintenance and later phases of program renewal are still being worked out in practice.

An early philosophy underlying the approach cautions universities and colleges to recognize the continued needs of communities in their region.[18]

> The college in the field should always tend its fences. It should have a follow-up policy. It should keep contact with the communities where work has been done. This need not be costly. An occasional visit, the loan of a resource man, a counseling service, the loan of a documentary film or packet of books, a requisition for cooperation in some other community, may be enough to keep the fire burning. The work in any case should go on. The entire area within the range of the college may become one continuation school. The time may come when communities as well as individuals will be proud to be alumni of the universities.

Consultant Models

Since research into the nature of the two models was restricted originally to publications, it left the question as to what extent many of these precepts were actually held to be important by consultants working in these communities. In an effort to bridge this gap, several interviews were held with consultants who had practical experience in working with each model. The interviews were conducted for the purpose of "finding what was important to know about the field of community development and community organization." The interviewer guided the discussion systematically into several subjects in which he felt the practitioners would especially be concerned.

The results of these interviews, combined with results from a questionnaire distributed to staff consultants, are described below, indicating what consultants from the two approaches considered most important on each subject brought to their attention.

Consultant Precepts for Community Action

Subject

Community Council Approach	*Self-Study Approach*

The Community Problem

The community is over-organized; there are overlapping services and unrecognized areas of need because social agencies tend to work separately and reflect narrow viewpoints.	The community is disintegrating; the small community is losing its strength, the large community is fragmented and depersonalized; the foundation of democracy is being challenged.

Definition of Community

The community is an area of common activity and interest, composed of public and private organizations which are interdependent in the total scheme of community life.	The community is more than a geographic area containing institutions; it is a concrete experience to be discovered by people who need to recover a sense of wholeness and by towns which need to recover an economic self-sufficiency.

Community Organization

Accept the local organizations as they are. If possible, bring together the separate groups into a representative council through which the effectiveness of each group may be increased. Do not create new organizations in an already over-organized community.

Accept local groups as they are but create an entirely new organizational structure to study the community; create new organizations if need be, to meet needs other groups are not meeting.

Involvement

Seek out top level leaders in each major area of community life who have leadership abilities and good knowledge of the community and enlist their aid in coordinating the work of public and private services.

Involve everyone regardless of their abilities or social background in a common effort to examine their community carefully to determine how it should develop in the years ahead.

Role of Consultant

The consultant should stay out of the spot-light. He should remain in the background as much as possible, encouraging citizens to take leadership. He should avoid too much personal involvement so that he can retain the objectivity essential to his work.

The consultant should become personally involved along with other local participants in working for the best interests of the whole community. Involvement is essential to the motivation of the whole study; he must become a symbol of the kind of leadership he expects others to take in community action.

The consultant must not provide an abundance of technical experts. He should not assume local responsibilities himself. Local people must be constantly encouraged to take responsibility themselves.

While responsibility for study and action is local, a consultant should endeavor to provide various technical experts to give helpful information; it not only gives people a measure of confidence in what they're doing, but a feeling of importance and dignity to their work.

Initiation

Begin the program quietly and slowly, becoming oriented to the intricate and unique situations as plans unfold. Start with small numbers and gradually build, knowing all the while, that the program is on solid foundation.

After preliminary talks, begin the program with full public support; make it possible for people to have drama, music, slogans, parades. Bring out as many people as possible to early town meetings; keep the record of attendance high throughout the program.

Techniques

Don't create a big publicity build-up of committee plans and raise expectations when it's impossible to tell whether a project will go through.

Provide the basis for a strong publicity program.

Long Range Objectives: Agency

Consultant should "work himself out of a job." As soon as possible the local program should be formed into an independent organization. At this point the consultant should leave and move on to other communities in need of assistance.

Consultant should not leave the community entirely. Frequency of visits may be reduced, but ideally a consultant should remain available for program renewal; the consulting agency has a continuing responsibility to the community in which action was initiated.

NOTES

1. *Community Planning for Social Welfare*, A Policy Statement (Community Chests and Councils of America, Inc., 155 E. 44th St., N.Y. 17, N.Y., 1950), pp. 4, 5.

2. *Organizing a Community Council*, "Report of a Committee of the Michigan Council on Adult Education" (Bulletin No. 330 published by Superintendent of Public Instruction, 1944), p. 6.

3. Walter L. Stone, *Community Welfare Planning and Organization* (Hanover, Indiana: Informal Education Service, 1949), p. 11.

4. *Neighbors Unite for Better Communities* (Community Chests and Councils of America, Inc. 345 East 46th Street, N.Y. 17, N.Y., 1956), pp. 10, 11.

5. *Teamwork in Our Town Through a Community Welfare Council* (Community Chests and Councils of America, Inc., 155 East 44th St., N.Y. 17, N.Y.), p. 7.

6. Stone, *op. cit.*, p. 9.

7. *Health and Welfare Planning in the Smaller Community* (Community Chests and Councils, Inc., 155 East 44th St., N.Y. 17, N.Y., 1945), pp. 14-16.

8. Stone, *op. cit.*, p. 14.

9. Organizing a Community Council, *op. cit.*, pp. 10, 11.

10. Baker Brownell, *The Human Community* (New York: Harper & Brothers, 1950), p. 4.

11. *Ibid*, pp. 114-15.

12. *Op. cit.*, p. 197.

13. Richard Poston, *Small Town Renaissance* (New York: Harper & Brothers, 1950), pp. 23-24.

14. Richard Poston, *Democracy Is You* (New York: Harper & Brothers, 1954), p. 11.

15. *Tool Chest for Community Development Leaders,* Pamphlet No. 1, Community Development Institute, Southern Illinois University.

16. Some of the material in this section is quoted, and the rest is adapted from *A Report on the Plans and Operations of the Department of Community Development* (Carbondale, Illinois: Southern Illinois University), pp. 9-16.

17. The remarks which follow in the next two paragraphs are the writer's own interpretation of functions which are only implied in the structure.

18. Baker Brownell, *The College and the Community* (New York: Harper & Brothers, 1952), p. 147.

CHAPTER 2

ACTION STORIES

How did action take place in each community?

Research Orientation

There were several different sources used in writing the case histories: (1) newspaper accounts; (2) consultant field notes; (3) interviews with local citizens and each consultant; (4) minutes taken of community meetings. After a chronology of events was outlined from local documents, citizens and consultants were interviewed, and a detailed description of what had happened was written and submitted to the consultant for what suggestions he might wish to make.

The writer sought to recapture something of the sentiment and attitudes surrounding the different local events in order to make meaningful as well as accurate interpretations in the later analyses. Three of the stories which follow are included in abbreviated form. The Eldorado story, however, is described at length for study in depth. The "development process" is interpreted later from this case on the basis of conferences with the consultant and local citizens.

ELDORADO COMMUNITY

General Characteristics

Eldorado is a town of 4,500 citizens (1950 census) located in Saline county in the southeastern part of Illinois, about 130 miles southeast of St. Louis, Missouri. A census taken by local citizens in the community development program recorded the population within the city limits as of midnight, October 24, 1954, as 4,075. This represented a loss of about nine per cent in the four-year interim. The reason was attributed to a closing down of the coal mines.

The community serves as a retail trading center for Saline County. It has a wide variety of mineral resources within trucking distance of town: fluorspar, zinc, lead silica, and various minerals for processing industries and construction. Existing in what has been labeled a "depressed area," industry had not been interested in making the initial capital outlay to develop the natural resources. The community contains a strong labor force; it does not claim to have a substantial professional and specialized occupational class. The median school year completed for persons twenty-five years and over was 8.4 years, according to the 1950 census.

Pre-existing Conditions

For many years the economy of Eldorado had been seriously unstable, the population had been declining, young people and capable leaders had moved away, and by 1953 the life blood of the community was fast being depleted. In former years nearly 2,000 men had been employed in the coal mines in and around Eldorado. Now there were almost none, and even the few coal mines that remained in operation were in the process of closing down. By the summer of 1953 the number of people moving out of Eldorado and its vicinity reached into the hundreds. The trouble was not limited to Eldorado, but spread over all of Saline County in which Eldorado is located and, indeed, over the whole of southern Illinois.

Coal mining, which had formed the economic backbone of Eldorado, and of the area of which this community is a part, had always been an up and down kind of industry, but now it was passing out entirely. In Eldorado more than twenty-five per cent of the labor force was unemployed. A spirit of defeatism had settled over the town and the majority of the people were dependent either directly or indirectly upon public assistance. No one in Eldorado had any idea of what needed to be done to improve the situation, except that somehow they ought to get in a new industry, and conversations up and down the main street commonly bordered on futility.

For many years the community had been divided into factions, bitter in their feelings toward each other, and it seemed impossible for the people as a whole to get together to work for any common goal. At one time the Chamber of Commerce had been effective enough to get the REA located in the Eldorado community, but that time had passed and now the Chamber of Commerce, like many other community organizations, was just barely managing to exist. Broadly speaking, the population of Eldorado consisted of a merchant class and a laboring class, neither of which had any respect for the other. Within these two broad groups there were many subgroups, all socially, politically, or economically divided against each other. This pattern of life in Eldorado had been in the making for more than half a century since the beginning of the coal mining industry, but with the drying up of the basic economy this social disunity and disorganization now left the community virtually prostrate and incapable of rising to the needs of the hour, even to save itself from gradual extinction. Physically, the community had long been in a seriously deteriorated condition. Educationally, the town was below both state and national averages. The population was deeply provincial in its over-all pattern of attitudes, and despite the drabness of the community as a place to live, the inadequacy of community facilities, and the numerous problems in every sphere of community life, the only internally felt need of the people was for a new factory or some new economic development that would provide the unemployed workmen with new jobs.

In many respects the situation was more hopeless than even the people themselves realized, for the town was in such a condition both physically and socially that there was little likelihood of any industry giving this place any serious consideration as a possible plant location. From the standpoint of the plant location requirements of modern industry, Eldorado had little to offer in comparison with other communities, either economically or as a place to live.

The First Sign of Hope

Early in August, 1953, an insurance salesman and an unemployed coal miner were discussing the critical and unpleasant
topic of their community's future in an Eldorado barber shop.
The question on the lips of everyone was, "What's going to
happen to Eldorado?" The obvious answer: "It'll never be the
same again." Although this particular barber shop conversation
was moving in the usual pessimistic vein, this time a spark of
hope entered it in the form of a comment from the insurance
salesman, "If you fellows would get busy and try maybe you
could get something in here." (It may be noted that people
never said "we"—it was always if "you" or "they" would do
something things might be changed.)

That "something" that the insurance salesman said the coal
miners might "get in here" was clearly a felt desire on the part
of all the people in Eldorado; indeed, the only universal feeling
they had. It was new industry. This desire for new industry
was not only felt by the citizens of Eldorado, but by the citizens
of all the communities in the southern Illinois region. New
industry—a symbol of the good life—was looked upon as the one
thing that could save a depressed community. It was the heart
of the community; if it was not operating well, or not operating
at all, it became a matter of sheer survival for every resident.
There were no large metropolitan centers in southern Illinois
to and from which people could easily commute to gain a living,
though many Eldoradoans drove 120 miles each day to work
in Evansville, Indiana. However, in this southern region of
separate, small mining communities, jobs had to be found locally
for the most part, or not at all. Without mines people could
not work; without work, people could not much more than
exist. They could live, but that was about all—from public aid.

It was in this kind of a social climate that the unemployed
coal miner of the barber shop conversation went to talk to his
friends, other unemployed coal miners. One of them, a leader
among the miners who had served time in prison some years
before for dynamiting a mine during a strike, and who had a
rough reputation among the town's more socially respectable,

suggested that they call a special meeting of all "workin' people" and see what they could do to bring new industry to Eldorado.

Labor Organizes

This meeting was held on Sunday afternoon, August 23, 1953, in the City Hall, and nearly a hundred people came out. At that meeting a new organization to be known as "Labor's Association for Industrial Development," which the people called LAID, was organized for the single purpose of attracting new industry to Eldorado. The ex-convict was named president, and other officers, consisting mostly of former coal miners whose reputations in town were almost as bad as the president's, were elected. Although the majority of LAID members were from the "working class" (many of whom were men the more "respectable element" of the community would have been glad to see leave town), there were a few businessmen, some politicians, and a sprinkling of housewives who included themselves in the group. LAID was not without support, though the bulk of its support was from the town's laboring class, and many people from the business and professional groups in the community would have no part of it. The new organization had the complete backing of the *Eldorado Examiner*, a newspaper published twice weekly, but received only mild support from the town's daily paper, the *Eldorado Journal*.

At the second meeting of LAID on August 30, 1953, the organization came to an impasse due to the fact that no one had any suggestion to make as to what specific steps the organization might take to get new industry. Here was a new organization established for the single purpose of getting a new factory for Eldorado, but no one could suggest how it might go about accomplishing that purpose.

Conditions at the University

Meanwhile, in the summer of 1952, a year previous to the organization of LAID, a Division of Area Services was organized at Southern Illinois University. A major part of this division was to be a department of community development for which the University was to obtain the services of Richard W. Poston as director. The purpose of this administrative reorganization was to extend services and resources of the University into the southern Illinois area to help improve the quality of living.

Early in September, 1953, shortly after LAID had been organized, a press release was issued by the University announcing the arrival of the new director of the Department of Community Development. This press release was printed in both Eldorado newspapers. At the meeting of LAID on August 30, both newspaper editors suggested that a letter be written to Poston requesting him to come to Eldorado and assist the organization in its quest for industry. This suggestion was adopted immediately, and on September 15, 1953, the day that Poston arrived in Carbondale, he found a letter from the secretary of Eldorado's LAID waiting on his desk.

How the University Program Began

Having just arrived from Seattle, Washington, where he had guided a similar agency at the University of Washington, the new director fully realized that he was in no way prepared to begin field operations immediately. At that time he had virtually no knowledge of southern Illinois.

He considered three alternatives as to how he might launch a program to upgrade and improve community life in southern Illinois. This was an enormous job, and the alternatives had to be weighed carefully. In simple terms these alternatives were as follows:

(1) Do not attempt any field operations for at least a year, but devote this time to a careful analysis of the area's conditions and characteristics, and on the basis of the findings of such a study determine how best to proceed.

(2) Organize a regional advisory group of leading citizens from throughout the area and in consultation with this group gradually develop a program for the area as a whole.

(3) Begin working in just one community and in this way establish a pilot project that will provide a demonstration, for the rest of the area, of what people in that community could do to improve local conditions from within. Such a demonstration

might provide some motivation for other communities and in this way local community development programs could be spotted throughout the area. Gradually, after enough such programs had been developed, there would be created what the director thought of as a "local foundation" upon which to build a regional program that would operate on an area-wide level.

He chose the latter alternative as his initial approach to the establishment of a community development program for southern Illinois. It was his feeling that no major change in the depressed economic conditions of southern Illinois could be made unless the problem could be eventually approached on an area-wide basis. He also felt that in this area it would be extremely difficult to establish any permanent local community effort for total community development until an integrated regional effort could be organized with the University's Department of Community Development functioning as the core of such an effort.

Eldorado is Chosen

With these thoughts in mind, the director decided to gamble on accepting the invitation from Eldorado. He decided that even though the recruitment and organization of a staff for the new department was one of the first essentials for the development of his program, it was also essential to establish an early demonstration that would make news in southern Illinois, which would in turn provide a new kind of desire in communities throughout the area. On this basis the director decided to devote as much of his own time as possible to a program in Eldorado for a period of at least six months. He decided further that in doing this it would be necessary for his long-range purposes in the area to make this first six months so spectacular in terms of news-making events that by the end of that period the new department would be (1) established in the public mind, and (2) the recipient of invitations from enough communities to make it possible to choose from the entire area the best possible communities for further activity that would provide the basis for a permanent regional program.

With this in mind, the director replied to the LAID letter of

invitation and suggested that a delegation of people representing a cross section of community life in Eldorado come to
the Southern Illinois University campus for a conference to
discuss the possibilities of a community development program
with the assistance of the University's new department. The
LAID leaders gathered together as many people as possible
to make the trip, a distance of fifty miles, and tried as best
they could to get a group that would be representative of the
entire community.

Before the delegation went to Carbondale, and before there
had been any contact between Eldorado and the director
(except by correspondence) LAID completed plans for a special
event in the community which at that time was unknown to
the director. On September 25, 1953, at a meeting of LAID,
plans were set for an outdoor mass meeting in the streets of
downtown Eldorado for the purpose of promoting LAID and
enlisting new members in the movement that LAID had started
to attract new industry to Eldorado.

On October 5, ten days after the plans for this LAID mass
street meeting had been completed, a delegation of twenty-
four people led by the Mayor of Eldorado and the President
of Labor's Association for Industrial Development went to
Carbondale to meet with the director and to make plans for
enlisting the help of the new Department of Community Development.

Eldorado Delegation Meet in Carbondale

The conference of this delegation of twenty-four and the
consultant, Richard W. Poston, lasted for five hours, during
which time he explained the concept of a total community
development program and the principles and purposes of community self-study. The consultant explained that the purpose of
community development was to enrich and improve the community in its entirety, that industrial development was only one
aspect of such a program, and that a program of this kind
would not work unless the entire community participated actively
and unless it was truly a program by, for, and of the community

as a whole. He told them that in order to be successful such a program could not be sponsored by any one special group, but would have to be sponsored by nothing less than the community, with the active backing and participation of all groups in the community: LAID, the Chamber of Commerce, the PTA, the Lions, the Women's Club, and all other volunteer organizations, the churches, and all official governmental bodies. It was emphasized that the basic aim of such a program would be total community renewal in terms of attitudes, human relations, understanding, faith, belief in each other, and all other interests of community life. It was pointed out how all this related to the requirements of modern industry, but it was emphasized that the central aim of community development is "community" and that the meeting of needs, whatever those needs might be, including economic, is all a part of that total process.

Some of the people in this initial delegation understood thoroughly what the consultant said and were enthused by this concept, which was new to them. Others did not quite understand all that they heard, but decided that even so, they ought to go along because they did need help from someone, and the consultant told them frankly that this was the only basis on which he would work with them. The entire delegation voted to accept the Department's offer of service on the basis outlined in the meeting.

The president of LAID asked the consultant if he would come to Eldorado and be the main speaker at the mass street meeting that LAID had planned for October 10. Thinking of the word "labor" as everybody, he assured the consultant that this would be a true community meeting, not a LAID meeting.

The Consultant Meets the Community

On October 10, 1953, the consultant arrived in Eldorado to find the main intersection in the heart of the downtown area roped off, with a speakers' platform set up in the middle of the intersection, a band playing, high school girls dressed in uniform, and a crowd of hundreds of people jamming the intersection. On the speakers' platform were seated the leaders of LAID and politicians from Eldorado and its vicinity. In front of the platform was a booth with a large banner soliciting $1.00 memberships in LAID. The consultant's previous feelings were confirmed. Whatever he might have said that day, the Eldorado Community Development Program would be considered by the whole community as a movement of LAID. But at this point there was no other course of action but to go ahead, and begin corrective measures later.

The consultant saw the situation as one which required rallying the community around the ideals of basic democracy and community-wide effort which were deep in the hearts of all the listeners, regardless of local partisanships. These were the ideals of American democracy, of the brotherhood of man, self-help, human freedom, the responsibility of individual citizenship in a free society, and of groups to work together for the common good. These were people who appreciated plain talk and spirited oratory; under a hot sun for forty-five minutes the consultant appealed to the people of Eldorado to forget factional differences and unite in one community-wide effort to build a stronger community by democratic methods. The speech struck home, and those present indicated their support by wild applause. One by one, other speakers on the platform supported the beliefs they had just heard expounded. There was no need for any official decisions to go ahead with the program; the Mayor simply arose and announced that T. Leo Dodd had been chosen as chairman of the new community development program. Then Dodd arose and gave an acceptance speech. The consultant met Dodd there for the first time. On their way home, the leaders of LAID and others who were a part of the delegation that met in Carbondale on October 5 had selected him because he was regarded as a natural leader of the community, neutral enough to move along the many factions of this community and to command their respect. Dodd had been a Baptist minister, a high school principal for fifteen years, and was well liked by most people in town.

With all its inherent risks, the Eldorado Community Development Program was now ready to begin.

The Self-Study Period

The program called for a comprehensive study of all aspects of community life by Eldorado's citizens. A large citizens' group would be formed to meet weekly. Out of this group a series of fact-finding committees would conduct surveys, identify problems and needs for change, and write reports of their findings which would form the basis for discussion at the weekly community meetings. The over-all program would be headed by a chairman, vice-chairman, secretary, and an advisory council. The advisory council was to consist of these elected officers, chairmen of the various fact-finding committees, and a few other persons to be named by the group. It was not, however, to be limited to study and discussion after which there would be action, but was to be study, discussion, and action all carried on simultaneously. This point was made clear by the consultant, even though he referred to the "initial study period"; for it was his belief that unless a certain amount of action could be generated fairly soon, the people in this community would fail to obtain any sense of achievement and it would thus be impossible to complete the study period. It was his feeling that during the first six months it would be necessary at least to complete the official study phase, and then over a period of several years, a more permanent type of program could gradually be established, especially as it became possible for his new department to move into a regional type of operation. It was also the consultant's belief that the social disunity and the public attitudes of defeatism and apathy in Eldorado were such that, unless the program could obtain early participation by large numbers of people and result in fairly dramatic action within a short period of time, it would be virtually impossible to effect needed changes in the community even over a long-range period; moreover, the Eldorado program would not provide the quick demonstration of local community effort that the consultant felt was needed to get the new Department of Community Development established in the public mind of southern Illinois.

The first step in actually getting the program organized was to conduct a survey to discover what the people regarded as their community boundaries. These boundaries extended beyond the city limits, but it was necessary to determine how far in order to define what constituted the "Eldorado community." The whole community was to become the unit of study. As soon as this had been done the next step was to take a complete census of population and housing of this entire community area, with local people doing the work themselves.

The Census

On the afternoon of October 10, 1953, following the street meeting, the consultant met with the chairman of the development program and other leaders in the program to begin making plans for the boundary survey, the community census, and a publicity campaign that would help facilitate the census taking. The following Monday, October 12, a special meeting of a few people was called at the high school to complete formal plans for organizing these first two surveys—the boundary survey and the census. By the end of that first week the boundary survey had been completed, maps were being prepared, and 180 people had been recruited to take the census. Following this, three-hour instruction sessions were held daily for two weeks to teach the volunteer workers how to take the census. This was a highly organized operation because the census was done in accordance with the same standards and procedures used by the U. S. Bureau of the Census in its 1950 census count so that the figures obtained would be comparable with the official figures of 1950, 1940, etc. The census was to provide valuable statistical data to be used in the study once the full community development program was organized, but its primary purpose was that of an educational instrument. In the process of conducting the census, 180 people would learn things about their community that they had never before realized, and the entire community would be watching for the results. This would also develop an early spirit of unity, get the whole community involved either directly or indirectly, provide people with an early sense of accomplishment, and help prepare the way for the full program yet to be organized.

From October 10 through the month of November the census provided Eldorado with one of the most intensive organized efforts that have been made in the history of that community. Throughout this period the publicity mounted, community interest increased rapidly, and the town became more and more improvement-conscious. Within this newly created climate many acts of improvement began to take place: for example, the Veterans of Foreign Wars got busy and provided painted waste receptacles on street corners throughout the downtown area. Interest in the possibility of a $252,000 bond issue for new construction on the town's three grade schools swelled, an interest that had never been present in previous school bond proposals. Virtually every organized group in the community issued statements to the effect that as part of Eldorado's new community development program they should all get behind the school bond proposal. This even included groups that had traditionally been opposed to any such move. It was during this period, the consultant later noted, that leaders first began to see something of the concept of the "process" of community development in terms of who was really to participate in this venture, and how everyone should become involved. From this point on into the middle of the year the program gathered a tremendous momentum of community-wide interest and participation, and throughout Eldorado people continously expressed surprise that such a movement was possible in what had been for so many years a sleepy and apathetic little town. For the first time in the memory of local residents, an over-all attitude of negative thinking had changed to a positive outlook toward the future.

The Consultant Moves Into Town

The consultant lived most of each week in the local hotel. He spent day and night talking to organizations, clubs, church congregations (which included sermons from the pulpit), informal gatherings; he accepted invitations to family dinners and talked with people in their homes, reaching into all levels of the local class structure, all the while talking about the importance of everyone being involved and having faith in working out the future of the community together. A good portion of the work during these weeks was to steer off any identification of the program with any one particular group in town. The majority of citizens knew that LAID was largely responsible for initiating the program, yet somehow they felt the impact of the consultant's and others' urgings for united action. Gradually, the consultant was overcoming the handicap of having the program labeled as a LAID affair. In fact, he later noted that, during these days he worked so hard to get people to realize that the program was not simply a LAID program but truly a community program, the LAID leaders became slightly hostile and wanted to know if he was ashamed to be associated with them. It then became necessary for him to spend extra time with them in order to satisfy them that this was not the case and to help increase their understanding of the meaning of "community."

The consultant established very close personal relationships with people in all levels of the community, and gradually the program did come to be regarded as an activity which included all Eldorado. Still, there were a few leaders in banking and commercial circles who did not participate whole-heartedly. At no time did these people openly oppose the program, though for a few of this particular conservative group the program was entirely too "wild," and, of more importance to them, the local leadership was made up of men against whom they had been prejudiced for many years.

Public Relations for the Study Program.

The boundary survey and the census enumeration having been completed, preparations were now made for the organizational meeting of the main phase of the community study. The date was set for December 7, 1953. On that night approximately a thousand people, nearly a quarter of the Eldorado population, jammed Dodd Auditorium in the local high school, formally to launch a five- to six-month systematic study of their community. The enthusiasm expressed that night was literally tremendous.

By this time virtually every organization in town had published statements of support for the program in both local newspapers, the *Examiner* and the *Daily Journal*. Both papers carried page one banner headlines, photographs, and special cartoons supporting the effort. In many of the issues of both papers, and in every issue of the *Examiner* for months, community development activities comprised the bulk of the copy printed on the front pages. Meanwhile, the story of Eldorado's program was being picked up by papers throughout the entire southern Illinois area, and shortly the story was being published in the big dailies of Chicago, St. Louis, and Evansville.

The newspaper at Centralia, Illinois, labeled the Eldorado program "Operation Bootstrap," and immediately this term was adopted in Eldorado and by the press from Chicago to St. Louis and throughout southern Illinois. Certainly, there could be no doubt that the new program was now recognized by the people of southern Illinois, or that the director's objective of establishing the new department in the public mind as a basis for going ahead with long-range planning was being accomplished.

Town Meetings Begin

At the organizational meeting on December 7th, T. Leo Dodd was elected permanent general chairman. The mayor of the town was elected vice-chairman. Others were elected for the advisory board and as secretary and treasurer. That night, sheets of paper listing fourteen study committees, including discussion leaders and recorders, were distributed, and almost a thousand people signed up, indicating in which area of the program they would prefer to serve. During the next two weeks these sheets were used by the elected group and the consultant as the basis for designing committees, discussion leaders, recorders, rounding out the advisory council, and the like. Actually, the people present at the December 7th meeting had appointed themselves.

On December 14, 1953, the second "town meeting" was held in Eldorado High School, at which time the people filled out questionnaires on the "character" of their community. This included questions pertaining to values held by the people of Eldorado and to factions and groups in the community, the relationships among various groups and the effect that such matters had on the community's ability to solve its problems or accomplish significant goals, what they liked and disliked most about their community, what they regarded as some of the most pressing needs, and similar questions. Five hundred and sixty-two of these questionnaires were completed. The results were tabulated at the University and written into a report with questions for discussion at the next town meeting.

This report was discussed at the town meetings which followed at weekly intervals, despite the Christmas season, on December 21 and 28, with the people divided into "buzz sessions," each with its own discussion leader, and with each group meeting in a separate room of the high school. After the discussion period, which usually lasted for an hour and a half, the buzz groups would reassemble in the auditorium, where the recorders would report to the entire assembly the conclusions and rec-ommendations reached in their respective discussion groups. This became the pattern for most of the weekly town meetings, though a few later meetings were conducted on a panel-forum basis. Even though the consultant suggested that they suspend the meetings during Christmas holidays, the study group voted unanimously to continue meeting without interruption. Several hundred people attended regularly through this season.

On January 4, 1954, the town meeting was based on a rating scale pertaining to what the consultant referred to as the "level of community maturity." The people, meeting in buzz sessions, first checked the rating sheets, then discussed the reasons for their rating. As a result, there was a widespread expression of increased community understanding, unity, and a new sense of confidence in Eldorado. In meetings many people openly expressed their enthusiasm with what they referred to as "learning to know each other" and "learning things about the community we had never thought about." Gradually, people were beginning to see some of the basic reasons why it had always been so difficult in Eldorado to solve any problem, including the need to strengthen their economy.

For the next regular weekly town meeting scheduled for

January 11, 1954, it was planned to get the various study committees organized so that the committee fact-finding work could go forward. For this reason it was planned that instead of breaking the large group into buzz sessions as had become the established custom, the large assembly would be divided into committee groups according to the preferences that had been indicated at the organizational meeting on December 7, or that might be expressed again on January 11. Meanwhile, chairmen for all committees had been selected by the officers and advisory council, and the consultant had met individually with these committee chairmen to supply them with study materials and to help them understand clearly their jobs.

He knew that, with fourteen committees all meeting at the same time at the town meeting scheduled for January 11, it would be impossible to spread himself among all of them. For this reason he decided to bring in fourteen specialists, one for each of the committee areas, to sit in and help the committees learn how to go about doing their jobs, including the gathering of pertinent data for their reports which were later to become the subjects for discussion at ensuing town meetings.

There was one serious disadvantage to this technique of bringing in fourteen specialists, which the consultant had learned from previous experience in other committees where he had worked in the West. These people, while well-informed in their subject matter areas, would have little or no understanding of the broad concept of community development, and hence could not be expected to be able to help the people of Eldorado see how these fourteen study areas were interrelated. This meant that after that first meeting of the committees the consultant himself would have to go around to all the committees before they could be expected to understand thoroughly how their work was to be integrated into the over-all program of community study and action.[1]

All kinds of devices were used to draw attention to this January 11th meeting; the result was that a little more than nine hundred people came to the auditorium. There was a general expression of satisfaction at the meeting according to the evaluation sheets that the consultant distributed that night.

He felt that it was reasonably successful, despite the necessity that he felt to meet with each of the committees himself. This is one of the many indications of the enormous amount of work that the consultant felt was necessary to help a community like Eldorado make a sufficient start in community development.

Summary of Subsequent Meetings

Town meetings were held in the months ahead in the following order:

January 18, 1954—*A special discussion* on a proposed purchase of the local water works, an immediate, burning issue on which the whole town surprised itself by engaging in what local residents regarded as a rational discussion, highly unusual for Eldorado on controversial issues.

January 25, 1954—*Report of the Population Committee*. Results of the Census.

February 1, 1954—*Report of the Community Organizations Committee*. A study of the organizational life of Eldorado and the relationship of this to the community's ability to get things done.

February 8, 1954—*Report of the Church Committee*. A study of the churches and their role in the general life of the community.

February 15, 1954—*Report of the Government Committee*. A study of local government problems, the structure of local government, needed municipal facilities, and possible ways of obtaining such facilities.

February 22, 1954—*Report of the Agriculture Committee*. A study of opportunities for increasing agricultural productivity, and current problems to be overcome with suggested possibilities for accomplishing the same.

March 1, 1954—*Report of the Industry Committee*. A study of opportunities for new home industry and of requirements that would have to be met to work effectively for the attraction of outside industry. A survey of industrial potential and of what specific types of industry Eldorado is suited for. A study of limitations.

March 8, 1954—*Special town meeting* on the community's need for a new sewage disposal plant. Limitations and possibilities. City Council held its meeting on the stage in the high school this evening so the whole community could participate.

March 15, 1954—*Report of the Trades and Services Committee.* A study of consumer buying habits, the status of the shopping center, possible ways to improve.

March 22, 1954—*Report to the Beautification Committee.* A study of the community's physical appearance and possible ways to improve.

March 29, 1954—*Report of the Education Committee.* A study of the community's public school system and problems needing attention.

April 5, 1954—*Second Report of the Education Committee.* The report of this committee was divided into two parts for two town meetings.

April 12, 1954—*Report of the Library Committee.* A study of local library services and ways in which they could be utilized in order to make a greater contribution to the community. Also, needed improvements in the library itself.

April 19, 1954—*Special Town Meeting* to discuss merchandising in the town and plan a special Eldorado Home and Style Show.

April 26, 1954—*Report of the Social Agencies Committee.* A study of social welfare problems in Eldorado and possible means of a solution.

May 3, 1954—*Report of the Health Committee.* A study of public health needs and resources, and possible ways by which specific problems in this area might be solved, and their relationship to other areas of community life.

May 10, 1954—*Report of the Recreation Committee.* A study of recreation needs in Eldorado for all ages in all seasons and the relationship of this aspect of community life to the general quality of living, with recommendations for action.

May 17, 1954—*Report of the History Committee.* A study of the historical development of Eldorado with emphasis on the origin of present day problems, and suggestions as to what might be the future history of the community.

May 24, 1954—*Special town meeting* to bring the study period to a close and discuss possible ways of going forward with an action type of program. This would be carried on by the various established organizations in the community, with some organizational machinery by which community-wide meetings could be held to discuss projects of community-wide importance. At this meeting it was decided to organize what was known as the Eldorado Community Development Association, or "CDA." For the time being it was decided to hold monthly town meetings instead of weekly meetings. Later these meetings might be held only as they might be considered necessary.

At this point the consultant announced that the pressure of work would not permit the University to continue working with Eldorado on as intensive a basis as had been the case up to this time, but that he would still visit them from time to time as the needs might dictate. Plans were also made at this meeting for a special community event to be known as "Band Wagon Day" to celebrate the end of the community study and the beginning of a less intensive, but more long-range type of action program as projected through the CDA. This was the last regular weekly town meeting.

June 19, 1954—*Special meeting to prepare for Band Wagon Day.*

June 21, 1954—Band Wagon Day celebration

June 22, 1954—Special Committee action

June 23, 1954—Park Construction

June 24, 1954—Special Committee action

June 25, 1954—Special Town Meeting

Filming of the Edward R. Murrow CBS Television Show on the "Eldorado Story" for "See It Now" to be carried nationally in October, 1954.

June 26, 1954—This date marks the end of what might be referred to as the "Study Phase" of the Eldorado Community Development Program.

With this schedule of events in mind, it now becomes important to go further into detail with regard to certain events in this study phase since they are a key to understanding the whole program.

Review of Major Events of Self Study Period

During the period from December 7, 1953, to June 25, 1954, which marks the "Study Phase" of the Eldorado Community Development Program, there was a wide variety of action and special events. It was a sudden creative release for the community. Some of these events which indicate the kind of movement that was underway are as follows: Financial contributions to the program poured in from organizations throughout the community, including $500 from the City Council for use by the Beautification Committee; local radio programs supported the development program with special commercials; the Junior Police helped direct traffic for the town meetings; a special baby-sitting service and nursery were established for children in order to permit their parents to attend the town meetings; free taxi service and school buses were made available to bring people to the high school for the town meetings every Monday night; various organizations staged parades and special events to help swell the town meeting attendance; the Eagle's Lodge staged a covered wagon parade; banners were placed across the main streets calling attention to "Operation Bootstrap"; cartoons were placed in the local newspapers illustrating the meaning of "Operation Bootstrap." And there were many other such events which resulted in virtually the whole town being involved for the first time in its history in a single concerted effort to improve itself and to build a better understanding among the people.

Action for Better Schools

Action for better schools that grew out of the program developed as follows:

On December 8, 1953, the Lincoln P. T. A. wrote in the local press, "As you know Eldorado has launched a development program that has as it purpose the improvement of living of all its citizens . . . what better beginning can we make than the improvement of our schools. . . . With united effort we can realize better schools for better children and a better community."

On December 10, the Jefferson P. T. A. said, "Surely here in Eldorado where we are striving to build a stronger community we can see the need to improve our schools."

The Washington P. T. A. said on December 15, 1953, "We must improve our schools so that when our town is being considered for a possible site for industry which we need so very much, our schools will be something to be proud of instead of buildings that are in such a condition that at least one of them has been condemned."

In rapid order other organizations through the community followed suit. The proposed school bond issue was discussed in town meetings, indeed at every community development meeting. Said the School Board, "There has been no major school construction for forty years." Only a year previous another request for new school facilities had been turned down, but this time the people of Eldorado were "community development conscious"; they were in a mood to act. On December 19, 1953, the bond issue carried three to one and at the next town meeting this was celebrated as Eldorado's first solid victory on what the local chairman of the development department called "the long road to improvement."

The City Hall is Renovated

At the town meeting on January 25, 1954, the Population Committee reported that nearly one-fourth of all the houses inside the city limits were without modern toilet facilities, thirty-three per cent had no bathtub or shower, and fourteen per cent had no kitchen sink. Other statistics on the housing condition were equally dark.

That night, in one of the buzz sessions, it was suggested that the people of Eldorado begin work on improving its housing by starting with its "community house," the City Hall, a building that was in a very dirty and run-down condition. In that buzz session, $50.00 volunteer labor and donated paint were pledged in a few moments. This was reported out to the town meeting general assembly when the buzz sessions reassembled in the large group after the discussion period that evening. The entire group of between seven and eight hundred people enthusiastically endorsed the proposal and the Beautification Committee was directed to come back two weeks later with a complete plan for the remodeling of the City Hall. Meanwhile, the Recreation Committee proposed that the third floor of the City Hall, which had been condemned because of structural weaknesses and which had been used for many years as a court room, be strengthened, remodeled, and fully equipped for a much needed "Teen Town." Plans were drawn up for this, including a Teen Town Board of adults and teen-agers to provide an ongoing program in the new facility once it had been completed.

Preliminary plans for the City Hall job were presented at the town meeting on February 8, and approved. At the town meeting a week later, February 15, final plans were in readiness, and on the morning of February 16, volunteer wrecking crews began tearing out the old front of the building. Thirty-five men worked in the rain throughout the day, and from that time forward until the job was finished it is estimated that nearly $30,000 worth of volunteer labor and materials went into the remodeling of the building, with a total cash outlay of slightly over $2,000. The workers on the City Hall included men, women, and children, and people from all levels of the population, working side by side on a common community enterprise. This was the first time in Eldorado history that local residents could remember an event of this kind. People in Eldorado recall how men who formerly had felt only disrespect for each

other learned during the action on the City Hall to know and
understand each other for the first time. The consultant called
it "one of the greatest learning experiences in the field of
human relations that I have ever witnessed." Each day Girl
Scouts served coffee and cookies to the workers. On the last
day, when the building was ready for its final coat of paint,
more than two hundred people, including the Mayor and the
entire City Council, turned out to complete the job. On April
25, 1954, a formal open house was held to dedicate what people
in Eldorado called their "new City Hall," and thousands not
only from Eldorado but from many communities in southern
Illinois came to see what had been accomplished. The newborn
spirit that was felt in Eldorado from this work is indicated by a
granite stone set in the new front of the building on which are
carved the words, "Democracy At Work 1954," a lasting symbol
of what "Operation Bootstrap" meant to this community.

Other Events

This spirit of physical rehabilitation spread rapidly through
the community, resulting in scores of homes being painted and
fixed up; the Eagle's Lodge was given a new modern front, and
a wide variety of beautification projects was initiated and
carried to completion. Special arrangements were made with
building materials dealers to help make it possible for people
to install plumbing fixtures in their homes, and hundreds of
abandoned outdoor privies were torn down. Landscaping was
installed around homes and public buildings where there had
been nothing but weeds before, and ten thousand golden daffodil
bulbs were ordered from Holland and planted throughout the
city. The name "City of Golden Daffodils" was unanimously
adopted at one of the town meetings.

At the town meeting on March 15 the Trades and Services
Committee recommended a Home and Style Show at which all
merchants in town would display their goods and services and
the clothing stores would present their spring ready-to-wear
on live models. In keeping with the community spirit that was
developing, and as a demonstration of the concept that all
segments of the community needed to have a real concern for

all other segments, this was not to be the usual type of commercial promotion by the merchants group but was to be an event planned by the community as a whole in which the merchants would simply take part. This was not a "merchant's promotion," but a project in "community education." The people in Eldorado were acutely conscious of the distinction, and the event was carried off over the weekend of April 23-24, with virtually the whole town turning out to participate.

Many other action events took place during the months of January, February, March, April, and May, but a description of one other should suffice to indicate the extent to which the Eldorado Community Development Program reached into all areas of community life.

Work in the Rural Areas

In connection with the report of the Agriculture Committee, the outlying rural area of the Eldorado community was divided into sections: Green Hill, Bixler, Cross Roads, and Raleigh. In each of these sections special meetings for the farm families were held weekly in the one-room rural school buildings. At first these meetings were planned to provide a means of engaging the farmers in a discussion of better farming and land-use techniques. However, it was found that it was virtually impossible to engage in an organized discussion. Farm people preferred discussion groups on a more informal basis, around coffee and cake. Most of these families rarely saw each other since rural gatherings in this community had long since ceased to exist. There had been nothing to bring these families together, either in rural churches or in any other type of farm gathering. The consultant remarked that the degree of inter-family communication in much of this territory was no greater than might be found in a large urban center.

The rural meetings averaged from fifty to one hundred people in attendance, separate meetings being held in each section. From these meetings was organized a series of farm demonstrations which were carried on with the help of an agricultural representative of the Illinois Central Railroad, representatives from the U. S. Soil Conservation Service, and a farm implement dealer at Ridgeway, Illinois. These demonstrations were carried on as follows.

On a given day the farm families in one of the four sections would assemble at one farmer's place and spend the morning having their soil tested by a portable soil testing laboratory of the Illinois Central. All the farmers would bring samples of their soil, and the technician would show them how to test it and tell them what elements it needed to grow better crops. At noon they would eat fried chicken which had been prepared by the women. In the afternoon there would be a demonstration of tree planting, pasture renovation, and other things that were of interest to the farmers. This aspect of "Operation Bootstrap" went on for several months, as a result of which several hundred acres of trees were planted on ground not suitable for anything else, improved farming practices were started, and, said the Soil Conservation Service agent, "More soil was tested in this area than we have been able to get tested in all the years we have been in business in Saline County."

Throughout the entire period of the study phase of the program, commonly referred to as "Operation Bootstrap," interest remained at a high pitch. Although attendance fell off at a few of the later town meetings, the average attendance for the entire period was close to five hundred, and at no town meeting were there fewer than one hundred people on hand for the discussions. It may be interesting to note in this connection that the two meetings at which there was the lowest attendance, and in which it was most difficult to get people interested, were the meetings on the program of the public schools and the library. Many people who did not attend the town meetings worked on committees and action projects.

However, despite the high level of interest and participation either in the various meetings, in committee work, or in the numerous action projects that took place, there was, underlying the entire course of the program, a restlessness over the deep-seated desire for new industry. Many people undoubtedly took part in the program because they felt that by doing so it would somehow result in the coming of new industry. Hundreds of unemployed men faced the expiration of their unemployment compensation checks, and as time went on there was no immediate promise of a new factory to keep them going. The consultant was deeply cognizant of this fact and knew that no matter how much community action might be accomplished it was only a matter of time before many of the "working class" would lose interest and drop out of the program if nothing could be done to supply new jobs enabling them to earn a living. Gradually, some of the most active, and many who were only moderately active in the program, were leaving for Detroit, Chicago, St. Louis, and other distant points, to seek work. This trend was inevitable in a town where widespread unemployment loomed over the population as it did in Eldorado.

Dealing With the Economics of the Community

Several moves were made to tackle this problem of unemployment directly. A home industry committee was organized to help start new small businesses from within. This was an extremely difficult thing to accomplish because it was of such a long-range nature, especially in this community where immediate action to provide hundreds of jobs was felt to be so tremendously important. As a result several committees were started for the purpose of creating small home industry, but none of them stuck. Two new small industries were started employing a total of six men as a result of the consultant working personally with both industries.

After the report of the Industry Committee, the Eldorado Chamber of Commerce, just barely existing at the time the community program began, was reorganized and reactivated. A detailed industrial resources survey was completed from which a comprehensive report was prepared to show industry seeking new plant locations what Eldorado had to offer in a factual manner. Slowly, the consultant moved through the Industry Committee and the Chamber of Commerce to organize an industrial development corporation, which later became known as the Eldorado Industrial Foundation, Inc., capitalized at $125,000. Several trips were made by the consultant and by members of the community to Chicago and cities in the East to contact corporate management on behalf of possible plant locations for Eldorado. Gradually, the basis for a long-range industrial development program was being prepared. However, it was always the consultant's belief that, even though it was worth making an effort, major industrial development would not be possible until a regional program was more fully developed, more facilities for this purpose were made available, and other ingredients essential to an effective industrial development program could be provided. It was his belief that, due to the competitive nature of modern industrial development, many major changes in the southern Illinois region would have to be made before the economy of this area could be substantially rebuilt.

The consultant maintained, "We had to start somewhere, and we had to start with what we had, and go gradually from there, hoping all the while that enough people in the area would learn what had to be done before interest fell off entirely."

The Television Show and Band Wagon Day

Then, in June, 1954, an unexpected opportunity presented itself which the consultant saw as the greatest single possible opportunity yet to present itself to satisfy the desperate need for new industry in Eldorado. A committee in Chicago which was laying plans for promoting adult education in America in preparation for the National Convention of the Adult Education Association of the U. S. A., to be held in Chicago in November, 1954, had thought of the idea of persuading Edward R. Murrow to do a nationwide television show on some program of adult education. In casting about for a program that might appeal to Murrow, they thought of the University's work in the Department of Community Development and telephoned the director to seek his reaction. He suggested Eldorado as a possibility. Two days later the consultant was in Murrow's office in New York City presenting the idea. Unfortunately, Murrow was not in the city at that time, but the consultant talked to one of the "See It Now" program planners and was told that as soon as a decision was reached they would notify him.

As indicated above, a special town meeting was held in Eldorado on May 24, 1954, to plan a special celebration of the completion of the study and to shift the program over to a less spectacular, but more permanent-type planning and action program. The plans for this celebration, which was to be known as "Band Wagon Day," with the theme, "Keep the Wheels Rolling," called for a large parade including thirty-six floats to be constructed by various organizations in the community. The town was to be decorated up and down the main street with wagon wheels and red, white, and blue bunting. The parade was to end at the high school where a special mass meeting would be held to review briefly all the committee's final recommendations for planning and action, and where the various organizations of the community could formally pledge their support to the newly formed Eldorado Community Development Association. Many special features were planned into this meeting to make it a memorable celebration. The idea behind the meeting was based on the consultant's belief that unless by some "crazy stroke of luck" a company selected Eldorado as a site for a new plant location offering at least a hundred new jobs within the fairly near future, the intense effort that Eldorado had been making to improve itself internally was sure to slow down markedly as soon as summer arrived. He fully expected to continue for as many years as necessary to help Eldorado ultimately find a solution for its economic problems, but the less the program slowed down, the easier and sooner this could be accomplished. For this reason he felt that Band Wagon Day should be of such magnitude as much as possible to impress on the Eldorado public mind the need for persistent long-range effort. And the plans for this celebration were made with broad strokes and on a very substantial scale.

The consultant related these plans to Murrow's representative in considerable detail and described what had been going on in the program thus far. Also, at the Band Wagon Meeting the Mayor was to proclaim a local holiday at which time the whole town was to turn out to fill in a four-acre swamp at one of the town's entrances and build a new city park in its place. Plans for this project had already been completed by the Beautification Committee, within which this idea had been conceived.

The consultant's meeting in Murrow's office was on Friday

morning, June 18, 1954. At noon the consultant left for Geneva, New York, to fulfill a speaking engagement, but upon arriving in Geneva a call was waiting for him from Murrow's office back in New York City. They had decided to film the Eldorado Story for the nationwide CBS TV show "See It Now" and they expected to have a camera crew in Eldorado the following Monday, June 21, to begin the filming which would require that entire week. Here was the chance for Eldorado to get the kind of nationwide publicity that just might attract the attention of an industrialist who would consider it for a plant location. Eldorado could meet the requirements of any number of types of plants, and the consultant was convinced that better community relations and a better labor force could not be found anywhere in the country by any company.

He telephoned from Geneva, New York, to Eldorado to give them the news. Eldorado was electrified. The consultant told them he would be there on Sunday to rehearse the Band Wagon Meeting, and suggested that all plans be stepped up and enlarged. Business literally ceased in Eldorado. That evening, all day Saturday, and all day Sunday almost every adult citizen went to work on the preparations. Instead of thirty-six floats they built 136. Instead of a parade of five hundred persons, they planned for one thousand. Instead of fifty horses, they got one hundred. Instead of a few wagon wheels decorated around town they scoured the countryside and brought in more than four thousand old wheels. Every store within a radius of fifty miles sold out completely of crepe paper of all colors. The consultant arrived on Sunday afternoon for an emergency meeting in the City Hall at which the crowd was so large that many could not get in the building. That evening they rehearsed the ceremonies that were to be held in the mass town meeting on Monday night.

On Monday morning, June 21, 1954, Eldorado was poised for the arrival of Edward R. Murrow's camera crew from New York. The crew arrived about noon after renting a truck to carry its equipment from the airport at Evansville, Indiana, and immediately went to work filming scenes in Eldorado. The downtown section was decorated in gala colors, hundreds of flags were flying, and thousands of wagon wheels wrapped in crepe paper; many of them, set up with electric motors that kept them turning, were mounted throughout the community with signs, "Keep the Wheels Rolling." The Band Wagon Parade began that afternoon and was so large it took nearly an hour and a half to pass any one point.

Never in the history of Saline County had there been an exhibition of anything on this scale. Thousands of people, many more than the population of Eldorado, jammed the town, and at the special town meeting that night it was estimated that at least three thousand people were jammed in and outside the high school. Nearly 1,500 were in the auditorium, which seated between nine hundred and one thousand, the overflow standing in the aisles and around the walls. Loudspeakers and benches were set up for the crowd outside, and that night Eldorado climaxed its Band Wagon Day. It is said that even now there is no one in this community who has forgotten that event, and many say they never will. Meanwhile, Murrow's cameras filmed the activity as it unfolded.

The next day, special committee action projects and meetings were filmed throughout the city. At dawn on Wednesday men with heavy road-building equipment moved on the four-acre swamp at one of the town's entrances. By that evening the swamp had been filled with 385 truckloads of dirt. More than five hundred residents, men and women, businessmen and laborers, had raked it smooth and planted grass seed. A park had been built in a day. Unfortunately, the grass seed didn't grow because it was too hot, the ground was too dry, and they had no way of getting enough water in to do any good. But no one was disappointed. This, along with landscaping, they could do later.

That day, while Murrow's cameras filmed the park under construction, Eldorado's $11,500 fire truck was destroyed while being used to put out a blaze in a nearby wheat field. The town fathers were appalled at the loss, especially since no insurance had been obtained to redeem it. But the fire in the wheat field was matched by that which was burning in the spirit of the day, and immediately efforts were made to raise funds for a new truck from voluntary donations. The money was pledged and gathered in full within the week!

On Thursday there was more committee action for the Murrow cameras, and again on Friday other action projects were filmed. Then, to make the show complete for the cameras, two thousand people came to the high school that night to re-enact a typical town meeting such as had been held during the study period. However, they did not just re-enact a meeting from the past. That night Eldorado held one of the most effective and constructive town meetings it had held yet, and the people demonstrated to the delight of the Murrow camera crew that they had learned some skills in group discussion and problem-solving techniques. It was that night that plans were completed for buying a new fire truck, and for further action to solve their housing problems.

With this meeting no further events were planned for the Eldorado Community Development Program for the rest of the summer, except for two outdoor town meetings, one in July and one in August.

It may be safely said that this week-long period was the peak of the entire development program in terms of community-wide participation. Leaders claim that not one person within miles around could have possibly missed being aware of the television show or actually being in it. The nearby town of Raleigh was said to have contributed four hundred people itself to the masses gathered on Band Wagon Day. Band Wagon Day symbolized the end of "Operation Bootstrap" and the beginning of the CDA (Eldorado Community Development Association). It is significant to note the change at this point. For six long months the sentiments of the community had been brought to a level no one would have believed possible.

Even the consultant, for all his personal optimism, felt that such a pitch of enthusiasm could not be maintained and that it would be a mistake to try. He felt that things should quiet down during the summer, and that in the fall they could begin again, with a different tone. The lethargy of Eldorado had been broken. Now was the time for the whole movement to settle down to a less spectacular, more modest, long-range type of program. Further, the consultant now felt that he should turn his attention to building his department of community development so that other consultants could move into other communities. Only then could preparations be made for the regional level operations he had envisioned.

Change of Pace

Despite the deliberate and inevitable slowdown after Band Wagon Week, a number of smaller action projects took place that summer: the CDA held two well-attended outdoor picnic meetings, and the new Advisory Council and official organization was greatly stepped up, and the newly reactivated Chamber of Commerce grew considerably in strength. This was a different type of community action than that which had characterized the Bootstrap days, but because it was different does not mean that the impact of the community development program had been dimmed. What was happening now was simply that the normal channels of community action were beginning to function as they had not been doing prior to community development. Action projects developed within the conventional organizations of the community.

In virtually every organization and club, plans and discussion centered on that organization's or that club's responsibility in the community development program. The CDA did not have a delegate from each of these established groups; indeed, the relationship between CDA and the normal organizations of the community was a very informal loose one. However, Eldorado citizens had developed a remarkable degree of unity. This was true to such an extent that practically anything that any group did came to be regarded as simply a part of the over-all community development effort. It was this notion of community effort, not the CDA organization itself, that was important.

An example of this is in the two tennis courts that were built during the summer by the Lions Club. Everyone in town knew that this was a Lions Club project, but in the climate of community spirit that Eldorado now had, the tennis courts were regarded as just another part of the total community development effort. In fact many non-Lions, including people from LAID, helped do the work. Another example is the Illinois Central Railroad painting its Eldorado shops that summer at the request of the Beautification Committee. Even though this work was done entirely by the paid workmen of the Illinois Central, the people of Eldorado regarded this as another routine part of their community development program.

The Community Development Association

In September, 1954, the CDA held its first large town meeting of the season with the consultant back from a summer absence to help kick off the fall work. That month they launched a community-wide "Alley-Rally," during which all the alleys in town were cleaned thoroughly and graded, and more sheds, which no longer had any use, were torn down. Block parties were held throughout the city as part of the program to help continue the increased closeness of human relations which had developed during Bootstrap days. In October numerous other action projects were carried out and the CDA committees were as busy as ever making plans for further development.

On October 12, 1954, the Eldorado Story was shown to a nationwide TV audience over Edward R. Murrow's "See It Now." The change from the type of activity that had characterized the days of Operation Bootstrap to the action of a few people in special groups such as the Chamber of Commerce became more pronounced, though CDA continued to remain the focal point of all Eldorado activity. The reason for this was that the consultant himself had decided to divert almost the total time— now much smaller than before—that he had to spend in Eldorado, to the specific purpose of finding a new industry for the community. This was due to the fact that in the closing scene of his "See It Now" show on Eldorado, Edward R. Murrow had made a direct appeal to American industry by saying,"If you are looking for a place to locate a new plant why don't you have a look at Eldorado. Just write or wire Operation Bootstrap. We repeat, Operation Bootstrap, Eldorado, Illinois."

Immediately letters began pouring in from all over the United States. Since he had brought the Murrow Show to them, the consultant now felt it was his obligation to the community to help them organize specifically for this particular purpose, and to help them weed out the hundreds of "fly-by-night" firms that would inevitably try to take advantage of them.

Later Developments

Hence, the consultant concentrated his efforts on strengthening the Chamber of Commerce, the Industry Committee, the LAID, and CDA Advisory Council, and on fusing these four into one specialized effort to deal with industry. During November, 1954, the consultant pressed for the completion of the Eldorado Industrial Foundation, Inc., and the raising of funds to subscribe its capital stock. In a single day the members of LAID moved into a large room donated by the VFW and converted it into a modern, painted, Chamber of Commerce office. Industrial brochures were printed and paid for up to $900. Five hundred copies of the economic resources report were reproduced. A paid Chamber of Commerce secretary was employed and permanent files were set up.

Meanwhile, the consultant brought in another staff member to help strengthen and extend the farm program, which that summer had resulted in rural road signs, many cleaned out fence rows, and a new addition onto the Bixler School. During November more community-wide clean-up programs were carried out, and businessmen were organized to sweep systematically the downtown streets every morning and evening. In December the Jaycees, formed as a result of the community development program, made elaborate plans for Christmas decorations throughout the city. Special industrial sales committees were organized to handle industrial leads. A Christmas flower show was planned and carried out. Plans were made for an all-out effort to get merchants to modernize their store fronts. The activity at this point, though being carried out through many separate organizations along with the CDA—very different from what had been the case during Operation Bootstrap days—was nonetheless equally intensive; indeed, far more intensive than the consultant had ever expected it would be.

In December he brought in sales development representatives

from Kawneer Metal Company, private architects, and store front dealers ranging from Evansville to St. Louis. Special meetings were held with the merchants. A detailed Christmas Shopping Habits Survey was conducted to establish the fact that local merchants were losing money which they could hold by certain changes in merchandising practices and store modernization. Finally, in January, February, and March of 1955, these efforts to physically rehabilitate the town began to get results. New store fronts went up in a dozen downtown buildings, three new buildings were constructed, and stores all up and down Locust Street began to paint up and clean up. The consultant felt that if Eldorado was to make good on the opportunity of a new industry that Murrow had provided through his nationwide TV show, it was essential that physical rehabilitation be undertaken and carried out as rapidly as possible.

Early in 1955, it was announced that Eldorado had been given the top award for American communities by the Freedom Foundation of Valley Forge for "its demonstration of the meaning of democracy in a free society." T. Leo Dodd, as president of the Eldorado Community Development Association, flew to Valley Forge to accept the award on behalf of the community. With him he brought home a gold medal and a Freedom Foundation check for $1,000. On March 14, 1955, Eldorado celebrated this event, and the community development program was going as strong as it had ever gone.

New Industry Fails to Materialize

The basic problem, however, was that the industrial leads gained from the Murrow show failed to materialize, and Eldorado was growing more and more hungry. In December, 1954, a small company called Cedaroma, which manufactured deodorants, was attracted, and two Eldorado men flew to Helena, Arkansas, to inspect the company. The delegation brought back a not too favorable report, for the owner was just initiating a relatively unknown product, and he was not sufficiently capitalized. Nonetheless, a few people thought it was a good opportunity to build something that had potential, and two men in the community, a dentist and the president of the Chamber of Commerce, advanced their personal funds up to $7,500. The new company moved into Eldorado on January 1, 1955. When the consultant learned of the advance of funds that had been made to the company he dropped all other work and came to Eldorado to audit the company's books personally. With the help of the new president of the Eldorado Industrial Foundation, Inc., he made a detailed investigation of the company, and found that the company had approximately $40,000 more liabilities that it had assets. Determined to do whatever he could to prevent the Eldorado men from losing their investment, the consultant worked with the owner of the company and personally arranged for sales outlets in stores throughout southern Illinois.

Unfortunately, it developed that the owner of the company was an alcoholic and a man with serious psychological problems. The consultant and his close friend Ralph Bedwell, director of Southern Illinois University's Small Business Institute, virtually took over the business, the consultant working with the company's owner, and Bedwell working with the business. It appears that the product had a good chance of selling on a nation-wide basis. Accounts were obtained with a number of large national sales organizations, and the consultant even went so far as to write to all the company's creditors and get them to hold off pressing for payment of the company's obligations until sufficient sales could be built to get the company operating on a sound basis. But production was not sufficient to meet shipment deadlines for the orders that had been obtained. Cedaroma had employed thirty-two people in Eldorado, and with this the people of Eldorado had hope in the midst of their severe economic plight. The consultant and a few people in Eldorado, with the help of Bedwell, did everything they could to keep the company alive, even to the point of meeting the payroll out of their personal funds one week when the company didn't have the money. Eldorado had to have jobs or its people could not live. Even community spirit, no matter how strong, could not long continue without a source of livelihood, and by now unemployment had climbed to nearly forty per cent of the total labor force. By the summer of 1955 Cedaroma went broke;

nothing short of more capital and a new management could have saved it. Thus, Eldorado's elation over its new industry turned to ashes.

Meanwhile, negotiations were in process with a foundry company from Chicago that offered a promise of employment for sixty men. This, too, went on for months but the company never located. The difficulty here was, again, lack of business. Other leads for new industry were pursued diligently, but nothing came of any of them.

By summer of 1955, Eldorado still had no new industry, though the carry-over enthusiasm from Operation Bootstrap days still held. But stark economic reality was gradually catching up. Here and there throughout the community the hope and faith of community development was beginning to break. The president of LAID had gone to Chicago to train in a new industry that had promised to locate in Eldorado, but this, too, failed to materialize. Eldorado wanted new industry so desperately that by now it was difficult for the people to keep going. Attendance at the CDA monthly town meetings was now beginning to fall off. Labor was falling away. These men could persist only so long. Then they had to quit the town for jobs elsewhere. And as they fell off, the businessmen tended to take over the effort. Labor was losing its leadership. The LAID president had gone to Detroit to work. Others had found it necessary to leave. The rank and file who remained lacked the staying power necessary to keep working. They left a vacuum, yet they resented the fact that the leadership was now shifting to business and professional people. They found it difficult to appreciate that this was due only to the fact that they were no longer as active as they had once been, and that the apparent control of the program by business was only a relative matter created by the absence of labor leaders.

During the summer of 1955, the consultant went to California to teach, and there was a dormant period in the Eldorado program. The pressure of economic necessity was now making itself felt more than ever. Eldorado was tending to revert to its condition prior to Operation Bootstrap.

The Art Center and Pottery-Making

While in California during the summer of 1955, the consultant came into contact with an official of the California pottery industry and learned that most of the clay used in California pottery comes from Mayfield, Kentucky, just about one hundred miles from Eldorado. He knew that he could not return to Eldorado and immediately start a new ceramic industry, but that it would be possible to start a new pottery making center for recreational purposes and that if this succeeded a new industry might then become a possibility.

The consultant knew from having studied geological maps that rich clay deposits lay only a short distance from Eldorado. He also knew that there were no pottery industries in all of southern Illinois, and that from a transportation point of view Eldorado would be an ideal place for a commercial pottery. That summer he went to Mills College and hired Gene Bunker, one of the best art potters in the country. In September, 1955, when the consultant returned to Eldorado, he presented to the CDA Advisory Council his idea for an **Eldorado Art Center.** The idea was received with great enthusiasm, and the next week at the first town meeting of the season he brought in Gene Bunker who demonstrated "pot throwing" on a potter's wheel. The crowd of nearly three hundred received the demonstration with marked approval, and voted to organize for the development of an Art Center. Bunker was detailed to Eldorado for full-time work.

A prospecting committee was organized and, with the help of a geologist from the Illinois Geological Survey, went to work. Soon clay beds were discovered, tested, and found to be suitable for high-grade pottery. Arch Baker, a local merchant, donated for a year rent-free an old church building that he had been using as a warehouse, and hundreds of Eldoradoans, in "City Hall Days style," moved in to put the building in shape. Ten potter's wheels and other necessary equipment, including a large Kiln, valued in total at $25,000, was constructed, and nearly three hundred people from throughout the community began to take part. A 450-foot pipe line was constructed to a gas well that went dry. Then a 1,500-foot line was constructed to another well, completed at three o'clock in the morning. Eldorado was working as intensively as ever for the development of the community.

By the spring of 1956 the Art Center had become an institution in the life of the community, and people were being trained for the time when it would be possible to develop a commercial enterprise.

Leadership Changes, But Attitudes Remain

During the late fall of 1955, the over-all community development program began to slow down despite the new art center development. The economy continued to go down; labor, with the exception of work on the Art Center, was continuing to fall away; and the businessmen were "taking over" more and more. Town meeting attendance was falling off badly, and although the consultant was deeply occupied elsewhere in the area and knew that it was normal for a community like Eldorado to go into a slump, he decided he ought to do something to prevent the slump from becoming too great. For this reason he dispatched two research assistants to Eldorado to conduct a public opinion poll from which a report could be written that could become the basis for a general reorganization of the Eldorado program early in 1956. By this time the consultant was building his department, and his administrative responsibilities were becoming so heavy that he had little time to devote to Eldorado.

This survey was completed in December, 1955, and showed that even though the majority of people in Eldorado were "hurting badly for the lack of industry," ninety-two per cent of the people felt that the community development program had been worth while and should be continued. A typical comment quoted from this public opinion survey said this, "You can't change a community in one or two or three years. Bootstrap can't bring industry in here until everyone gets his own house in order. This is a long-time job. It's an activity that should be continued. There should never be any let-up. It's a program of continual growth and development."

Recent Events

The early spring of 1956 was the last time that the consultant appeared for more than an occasional one-evening visit in Eldorado. The community went through the summer of 1956 in a fairly normal way but without the degree of community development activity that had characterized the previous two years. In June, 1957, a new president was elected to CDA. In the winter of 1957 the president resigned for reasons of business pressure. A new president took his place but in March, 1958 he died suddenly. Since that time to the present the CDA has not held any meetings.

In 1958 the Eldorado Industrial Foundation, Inc., raised $125,000 to launch the Eldorado Manufacturing Company, reconditioning valves for industrial motors. This company with twelve men employed at the present time has a potential employment of eighty men.

Meanwhile the consultant started working in the direction for which he had originally planned. In September, 1957, the Saline Valley Development Association was organized to encompass all of Saline and Gallatin counties. Eldorado played a significant role in initiating (and providing leadership for) this association which has continued to deal with the problems of the region. The association has established a conservancy district and provided the stimulus for the creation of a junior college; it is currently in process of studying the adequacy of highways and transportation routes in the region.

At the present time (1962) the community development program is no longer officially active in Eldorado. While no adequate survey of attitudes has been made for several years, close observers maintain that the community is confronting a period of calm reality in which the program and its activities are gaining perspective. The reality is that with all the community-wide emphasis that was given to the program some factional differences were never fully bridged. With all the unity that seemed to develop in the process a few individual differences were drawn sharper. With all the objective accomplishment of the program there were some who were disillusioned. The importance of some of these factors (and whether they could have been avoided) is still a subject of discussion locally. Those who were in the center of program activities believe what failed to be accomplished as unimportant compared to the progress that was made. They believe that the program left a legacy of human values, of organizational skills, and a philosophy of community development which will continue to work quietly to prepare the community for the challenges it will have to face in the future.

THREE SHORT STORIES

The stories which follow are abbreviated versions of what were formerly longer accounts made as part of the original research. They are included in this form principally to give the reader an orientation to each community and acquaint him with the sequence of certain program activities. These clipped versions cannot represent the cases fully or fairly and are necessarily subject to some degree of distortion. Many details essential to convey the significance which certain events had to local people—or to communicate the spirit of the work accomplished— have not been included. The result is an emphasis on the concrete problems and realities citizens must face in the operation of community action programs.

THE COBDEN COMMUNITY

General Characteristics

Cobden is an agricultural community containing a population of about 1,000. It is located in Union County which ranks high as a peach and apple area. There are various types of farms in the area: large fruit farms, several purebred Hereford farms, many small fruit and vegetable farms, field crop farms, general farms, and some farms devoted to large-scale flower production.

In addition to business establishments common to small communities, there are two mills which manufacture wooden packages for fruits and vegetables, two manufacturing concerns for corrugated containers of farm products, a large farmer's market, and a machine shop specializing in building special purpose machinery.

Much of the labor force in Cobden is seasonal. An average of 1,500 workers arrive in the community annually for the berry and vegetable harvest, and about 1,000 for fruit picking. These workers come on a temporary basis from southern Missouri and Texas.

Initiation

At the time of initial contact with Cobden the department of community development at the university was two years old. Its existence was coming to be known and its purpose explained by way of newsprint and dinner speeches. People in Cobden began hearing about it in the summer of 1955. At the request of the Cobden Lions Club, representatives from the university came to the community to speak officially, first to the Lions Club and then to other groups, about the nature of the program. Local citizens became convinced that Cobden needed such a program.

A delegation of citizens went to the university for detailed discussion and planning before the actual launching of the community development program. A census committee was selected and a general community meeting was planned to set the self-study program into motion.

Organization

Considerable local planning went into the preliminary meeting which was held early that October. Leaflets were dropped from airplanes. Loudspeaker trucks drove about town announcing the meeting. Four hundred people came to the high school gym to hear about the proposal. A panel of speakers (composed of university representatives and local leaders) was on hand to explain what the program was to be about. Preference sheets were passed around the audience upon which people could indicate their interests according to the list of fact-finding com-

mittees (agriculture, retail, beautification, etc.) which were to
be organized.

In the next few months organization took place rapidly: an
advisory council was selected, committees assigned, a community
characteristics survey initiated, and a program slogan selected
called "Operation Cooperation."

Execution

Weekly town meetings continued through January and February to hear and act upon the Census Committee report, the
Organizations report, the Trades and Services report, and the
Education report. During these months a chamber of commerce
was organized and a tomato co-op created as a result of the
interest generated within the fact-finding committees. There
was no clear distinction between what was technically called
the self-study phase and the action phase. Both were occurring
simultaneously. However, the leaders believed there was a
serious lag between the expectations built up at the launching
of the program and the accomplishments to date. By March,
they felt it was time to take some real action.

In March a "Holiday of Work" was organized, in part to
stimulate interest, but also to do a job that had needed doing
for a long time. At an appointed morning hour several hundred
people responded to the call of the fire-engine siren and joined
behind the marching school band to spend the entire day cleaning
up the community. Men and women from all sections of town
worked together cleaning streets, clearing rubbish from lots,
painting store fronts, bulldozing land for a roadside park. The
local newspaper called it a "colossal affair."

Still, some committees did not continue to develop as productively as the consultant and leaders hoped they would. It
was decided to organize a community council to construct
the program on a new basis. The council, once organized, went
on to support the annual peach festival, to aid in reorganizing
Teen Town, to organize little league baseball, and to nominate
officers for a new Industrial Foundation which would seek
appropriate means for new industry to settle in the community.

Maintenance

After a number of months the community council confronted the practical problem of a lack of attendance at meetings. Seldom, if ever, did the council have its full complement of official representatives from seventeen organizations in the community. The council problem can be explained in part by the fact that a few key leaders were asked to represent four or five different organizations in which they held overlapping membership. If a few of these key leaders were absent for some reason, the meeting was too small to act decisively. It is also true that a number of outside agencies which sought to activate interest locally in their particular projects did not seek to enlist the aid of the council but sought sponsorship elsewhere. Perhaps unaware of the council's existence or its purposes, these groups tended to organize new groups where none had existed before. There was no real evidence of interest in its existence. It seemed as though the third year would witness the end of the council organization.

Then suddenly the community confronted a new crisis. The local physician died. The council met to discuss the problem which was felt to be vital to the interests of everyone in the community. A vigorous campaign was launched to locate a doctor and to establish a clinic for him. In nine months of concentrated effort, with hundreds of people participating and donating money for the clinic, the project was completed. The clinic was dedicated on March 1, 1959.

A great deal of sweat and tears went into the clinic project. At the last meeting of the community council (fall, 1960) the nominating committee was unable to find anyone willing to take the official leadership in the coming year. For the last two years the council has remained inactive. The board of the industrial foundation (which was a creation of the council) is currently meeting on a quarterly basis and has business which will likely keep it going for some time. Whether the council itself will arise again at some time in the future is difficult to anticipate; but there is no doubt about its potential to rise to the occasion and contribute significantly to the welfare of the community. The achievements of the council and the community development program now have a permanent and distinctive place in the history of the Cobden community.

CHAPIN COMMUNITY

General Characteristics

Chapin is a small rural community of about five hundred population situated ten miles west of Jacksonville, Illinois. Its residents are chiefly descendants of the original German and English settlers who came there over a century ago. The U.S. Census bureau records the population in 1900 as 552; this number has not changed significantly over the years. A recent census tabulation shows an unusual number of older residents relative to other age categories.

There are two blocks of businesses, comprised of two grocery stores, a lumber yard, a carpentry workshop, a shoe shop, a bakery, a post office, a repair shop, a welding shop, a locker-plant, etc. The economic strength of the village lies in the Farmer's Elevator, the Midwest Order Buyers, and the Chapin Bank. A Methodist and Christian Church exist within the town limits; a Lutheran Church is located on the fringe of town. There is a grade school and a district high school.

There were numerous kinds of community problems that needed attention, which proved to be the basis for discussing the need for a community council.

Initiation

The idea of a Chapin community council began in the summer of 1950 when a staff member of the college program of community development began talking with local citizens about the way a community council may make it possible to deal with community problems. Since strong interest was manifested among several groups, it was decided to hold a town meeting to consider the idea. The meeting was held with thirty to forty persons attending and the idea was approved wholeheartedly.

The following month the council was officially organized and major projects for the community were discussed. The projects chosen by the council to act upon were: (1) obtaining a physician for the community, (2) establishing a public dumping ground, (3) making street improvements, (4) improving the town hall.

In the beginning the meetings were representative of the town, including laborers, ministers, farmers, Methodists, Lutherans, Christians, retired businessmen, widows, some well-to-do, others struggling to make a living.

Execution

In order to execute the projects successfully, it was felt that some initial funds and more general community support would be important to obtain. An auction was planned and held, attracting some three hundred people in the region and making over $500 profit.

Action then took several directions. Two of the council projects were completed rather quickly, as a farmer was moved by public interest to donate a section of his land for the dumping ground, and the Town Board was encouraged to paint the town hall and improve its appearance. The council then voted to donate $150 from its newly acquired operating funds to the P.T.A. to purchase band uniforms for the high school. To stimulate interest in developing recreation programs locally, a recreation training program was initiated with the aid of the consultant and a visiting team of specialists from a Northern university.

The problem of finding a doctor for the community was somewhat more difficult. The committee worked with medical groups and other agencies to locate one; fourteen doctors came singly to visit the community over the summer and fall months of 1951. For some time every effort of the council was channeled into this one project, but with no success.

In the spring of the following year attention turned to another problem, that of creating a small park out of an unsightly old lot next to the Fire Department. Farmers donated their equipment to clear the land; women completed the job of landscaping, planting bushes, grass, and flowers around the edges of the lot. When the Community Park was finally prepared, an ice cream and cake social was held to celebrate and raise more funds for council operations.

That summer some street improvements began to be made. A two-month long recreation program for public school children with time on their hands was initiated by the chairman of the recreation committee. The council officers continued to focus on obtaining a doctor.

In the late summer a doctor responded. A house was prepared for him and a general reception was held that fall. However, after a year the doctor decided to move to a neighboring community. All that year the council efforts had been spent seeking to make the doctor comfortable in the community and the move was met with great disappointment. Soon the doctor found the neighboring community not altogether what he was seeking and left there, moving out-of-state.

With this event the council meetings dwindled in attendance until few, if any, people came to the monthly meetings. Actually, it was said, the projects which everyone had set out to accomplish had been completed, with additional projects for good measure. The medical project was disappointing, but much was learned, and it was best to let it go for the time being. The scarcity of doctors for such small communities (it was reasoned) may have been too large a problem to solve with present resources.

A meeting of seven or eight persons composing the remaining nucleus of leaders was held and it was decided to terminate the existence of the council until the need for organizing was evident again in the future.

JACKSONVILLE COMMUNITY

General Characteristics

Jacksonville is located in west-central Illinois. The city was incorporated in 1840; in ten years, at mid-century, it had already become established as an institutional center with two private colleges and two state schools, one for teaching the deaf and the other for teaching the blind. The community continued to develop in this direction in succeeding years, adding a small business college, four private hospitals, and one state hospital (currently housing some 3,500 patients). In time small diversified industries also developed so that at present there are about forty small industries.

The population has remained stable for a number of decades, presently totaling about 20,000. The state capital, thirty-six miles directly east, draws a substantial number of the working population. The community has a large proportion of white collar and professional people who are interested in social welfare. This became the starting point for development of a community council.

Initiation

In the history of Jacksonville there had been several attempts to organize a community council but each had failed to move past the talking stage. There seemed to be a lack of understanding as to how to get started. There was clearly a concern among professional people about overlapping services and a lack of coordination among voluntary and state organizations. In a survey taken by college students it was found that over one hundred major organizations provided services to the community in different ways, yet with very little communication among them. At Christmas time ten or eleven different fraternal and church groups would take baskets around to the "less privileged" families. Without coordination of their work some families were overly provided with food and gifts for the season while others received nothing. And so the story went in various areas of community work.

The action program began in the summer of 1952 when several professional people talked with a staff member of the college community program about these community needs. Deciding to serve as a consultant for the initiation of the council, the staff member sought to stay in the background as much as possible. It was clear that the college was in competition with other organized groups, which meant that any strong public role the consultant might assume could be easily misinterpreted. The college had a public relations department and occasionally promoted fund raising drives sometimes described as "development programs."

A council of social agencies did exist with four members (the Salvation Army, the Boy Scouts, Girl Scouts, the YMCA) but met officially only once a year to elect members to the community chest board which then conducted a campaign on their behalf. The council of agencies met in a special session to consider the possibilities of a community council. After some deliberation with the consultant, it was decided to mail invitations to eighty or ninety organizations (believed to have social welfare services contributing to the community) to come to a town meeting to consider the idea together.

The meeting was held at the YMCA with about forty organizations responding. The group voted unanimously to approve the "idea" and appointed a committee to look into organization procedures. This committee met with the consultant, and a temporary constitution was written; temporary officers were nominated for the next assembly of organizations to consider.

At this second "town meeting" the officers were elected as a temporary "executive committee" and the constitution was discussed for representatives to take back to their organizations for separate approval. The new officers decided to hold a large dinner meeting at which time the constitution could be ratified and broad general support from the community could be developed. A well-known welfare speaker was chosen and the meeting was held with over one hundred people attending. They were people from all stations of life in the community, meeting with a feeling of inspiration.

Execution

Two months later the executive committee met privately in the home of the newly elected president. Committees were decided upon: membership, publicity, planning (with subcommittees in education, rehabilitation, health, welfare, and recreation). The chairman of the planning committee was given a list of thirty delegate names from the seventy groups (still in process of affiliating through organizational channels) to divide among the five subcommittees. Form letters were composed and sent out to delegates, informing them of their selection.

Briefly stated, these committees within the planning committee did not develop. It seemed at this point that leaders were more concerned about developing a council structure than about the interests of local citizens themselves.

Sensing the difficulty, the planning committee chairman called a town meeting to discuss major issues confronting the city. This meeting gave incentive to the directory committee, another committee appointed by the president, to develop a formal listing of the organizations serving the community and the nature of their resources. Compilation of the Community Directory involved considerable citizen effort and was completed with a minimum cost due to voluntary contributions toward printing and materials.

The consultant's academic responsibilities were increasing and, believing this latter effort to be an indication that the council was moving ahead, he decreased the frequency of his contacts with the program.

Maintenance

A year passed and the first annual meeting was held. The appointed committee chairmen announced their continued interest and promised that their committees would be productive in the coming year. Many months followed with no significant action. The president, superintendent of one of the local hospitals, sought to associate the council with the Community Chest. He reasoned that part of the problem curbing action was lack of staff assistance to keep contact with the organizations, informing them of activities and needs in the community. He secured several hundred dollars for the coming year. Then many more months passed as he too became occupied by added responsibilities forced upon him in his professional work.

A meeting was finally called among council leaders and

friends to activate interest and reorganize the council if necessary. It was decided to conduct a newspaper survey to determine public needs and arouse some interest. An ad was placed in the local paper with a clipping allowing space for citizens to write in needs as they saw them. More than three hundred citizens replied with every kind of idea imaginable, but mostly about their common discomforts: stated preferences for standard time, public toilets for shoppers, abolishing the wheel tax, eliminating stray dogs, better street lighting, etc. Many of these complaints (especially the physical problems) were not considered within the province of the council. Leaders referred them by letter to the city council or to the Chamber of Commerce. Although many were petty complaints which council leaders did not feel worth considering, there were others which could be discussed at a public meeting. As soon as the results could be tabulated, they were presented to a town meeting in which about forty delegates participated. The meeting divided into buzz sessions to discuss delinquency, housing, family welfare, and recreation problems which seemed significant from the survey. At that meeting it was hoped that a new president could be elected to start off the new year. However, no one could be found who was willing and capable of leading the organization. Finding no new leadership, the retiring president decided he had gone as far as he could without sufficient response and called no new meetings.

Investigation revealed that action did occur following the council's demise, as a delayed response to its public meetings. The YMCA held a week-long series of discussions on delinquency problems; the Council of Church Women held a community self-study program on youth, housing, and recreation; the League of Women Voters sponsored a critical community meeting on housing, inviting an official to talk on public housing; several meetings were held through local groups to discuss the initiation of a family agency. Leaders were able to urge the city council to adopt a building code which the council had brought to the attention of the community. *In each case, former council leaders were prime movers.*

The council had failed to take independent action on problems;

it failed to survive as a formal association in the community; but it had succeeded in developing a public sense of welfare needs through a series of four or five major town meetings. It created an informal network of social relationships which did continue to exist, working through established groups on the problems accentuated by council forums and publicity.

Consultant Roles

What roles did the consultants play in each community?

There was a different consultant working in each community and each had his own temperament and interests which affected the direction the community would take in following the ideal model. Some description of the background and professional values of the consultants is important for an understanding of their individual influence upon community events.

It is equally important to examine what principles were held in common among all four consultants. A by-product of this analysis will be the answer to this question: Is there a framework within which consultants perform their work regardless of the ideal model, the size of community, or individual temperament?

The Chapin Consultant

The Chapin consultant was a graduate of a school of social work at a prominent university. He had studied the philosophy and method of community organization and his interest in the community council approach was a result of this training. The following quotations are from private correspondence with the consultant in 1958 in an effort to obtain some understanding of the consultant's own point of view.

The consultant's view of his role in Chapin is described by him as follows:[2]

> My main function was to develop interest initially in community activities. There was latent interest, (which I feel is fairly universal) and latent leadership . . . the principal function of the consultant is to bring this out in the open and give it a

chance to run by itself. . . . The consultant's job will taper off as the group becomes organized and operating. Several of the projects you mention involved little or no work on my part. We talked them up as desirable projects during organization, and often I supplied mailing materials promoting them but this was about all. The band uniforms, town hall painting, street repairs, dumping ground, park clearing, summer recreation days, and other things would be included here. As a consultant, I was able to offer mimeographing and mailing services, clerical facilities, tabulating equipment, ideas and experiences other groups had, etc. In general, I just painted the picture that the Chapin group could achieve whatever they wanted to do, if they were willing to pitch in and work at it. If they stumbled, I would help them up again and they didn't feel alone or lost or bewildered at any time. But they really needed or called upon me very little after they got going.

Although he included labor in the initial stages of the Council formation, the consultant stated that he purposely placed an emphasis on upper level groups.

The Chapin group was more of an upper level group and I used people more accustomed to assuming initiative and responsibility. Still, before I started there, other towns felt it was hopeless and that Chapin was as dead a town and as stagnant as any place could possibly be. But with the labor groups, and low income groups, there is much more continuing leadership needed. That may be an unfortunate phrasing, since continuing work is necessary, but direct leadership is a pitfall to be avoided.

The avoidance of "direct leadership" and the emphasis upon "an upper level group" may be a result of training in the field of social work.

The Jacksonville Consultant

The Jacksonville consultant assumed the duties of the Chapin consultant in its second year. Believing the Chapin council well on its way as an independent group, he spent the greater part of his time working in other communities and with students studying these communities.

The roles of the two council consultants were similar in a number of ways. Both established regular informal talks with community leaders, both organized adult education conferences on the college campus, both produced radio programs which described stories of successful projects in the local area, both circulated publications in the region which aimed to stimulate interest in (and transmit knowledge about) community organization. This established their role on a regional level with less personal contact with single communities than was the case in southern Illinois.

Students worked with both consultants and sometimes aided citizens in taking action on particular projects. For example, one student was asked to talk to the Woman's Club in Chapin about the organization of community councils; another student volunteered to write minutes of meetings. In Jacksonville, students worked with citizens to collect data for the Community Directory. These activities were part of the field work associated with a course in Community which students were taking at the college. The emphasis on student education placed a greater responsibility on the community to create its own incentives to take action than was the case in southern Illinois. The student-teacher meetings within the community situation may be part of the explanation as to why the west-central consultants were more formal and indirect in their consulting roles than those consultants in the following two cases. A complete explanation, however, must include the character of community life and culture with which each group was working.

The Eldorado Consultant

The Eldorado consultant was serving as director of the newly established department of community development and had considerable experience in community work behind him in comparison with the other consultants. He was seeking, among other things, to establish a pattern of consultation for other staff members by demonstrating the process himself in this community. He recognized that Eldorado had its own peculiar qualities, and these were to determine major strategies in his approach to the people. This could be done, however, without changing basic principles which are important in dealing with any community.

The consultant's role in this case actually underwent considerable adjustment and readjustment, not only to contrasting personalities in this southern Illinois community, but to whole classes of people. The following incident occurred at a meeting with miners and other laborers early in the program:

> The discussion went on about how the miners should be a part of the whole community program, but class prejudice was constantly arising. An ex-miner spoke to the consultant about a so-called rich businessman who he considered threw his weight around town entirely too much. The program schedule called for them both to be on the same committee. The more the ex-miner talked about it, the more sweat poured from his brow; in the heat of anger at the thought of serving on the same committee with his enemy, he threw up his hands and swore he was through with the whole mess. As he turned to walk out of the meeting, the consultant impulsively jumped to his feet and caught him at the door. He spoke to the ex-miner in terms he could understand and asked him to sit down and listen for a while. The consultant talked about the importance of this program to the community in bringing its standard of living up to a point where people didn't have to starve, where men could obtain jobs again. The ex-miner listened and then decided to suffer the indignity.

An outstanding feature of his work was the intensity and commitment which accompanied his approach to the community. He encouraged a similar kind of commitment and belief among those citizens with whom he worked.

The Cobden Consultant

The Cobden consultant had considerable background in agricultural extension work at a university in a nearby state and was familiar with the community council approach before joining the staff. He came to learn about the self-study procedures during the initial stages of the Cobden program which had begun at about the time of his arrival at the university.

He was active and direct in his approach to the community,

making his position on local issues clear, supporting what he considered the best ideas brought forth by citizens in committee discussions. He wrote open letters to the village newspaper summarizing the program achievements, praising the community for work well done. He challenged people to do still more and outlined future directions which the community might take to deal with its problems.

An important objective in his approach was to create a situation whereby people could think for themselves. The self-study process was therefore ideally suited to this purpose.

Differences in Roles

The community council consultants worked primarily with community leaders; the consultants in southern Illinois worked more literally with the whole community. The former consultants established a public role in identification with the community council and were therefore in a different position than the latter, who were in a broader relationship to the whole community.

The role of the consultants in the two southern communities was more clearly expressed through public appearances before large assemblies of people. The consultants came into communication with great numbers all at once in speeches that spoke to people personally. The roles of the west-central consultants were less public or personal and more indirect in nature.

Similarities in Roles

The following outline shows certain features common to the roles of all four consultants. One may recognize differences in emphasis by each consultant, but the fact that these assertions are validly descriptive of all four cases is important to note. What can be seen emerging is a general pattern of principles and procedures which serves as a framework for community consultants. It allows for considerable individual variation but sets forth professional standards which practicing consultants on community organization set for themselves.

1. *Each consultant became oriented to the community.*

   a. Each consultant sought factual information about it.

   b. Each sought acceptance on the part of local citizenry before commencing work.

   c. Each sought to discover "community leaders" and enlist their aid in the process.

   d. Each searched for significant leads (with local citizens) to community problems which they encountered.

2. *Each consultant established primary relationships.*

   a. Each consultant attempted to establish friendly relationships with everyone with whom he came into contact in the community.

   b. Each found it important to clarify his role to local citizens in the beginning of the program.

3. *Each consultant developed new interest and understanding in the community.*

   a. Each sought to create an atmosphere where new ideas and individual initiative would appear.

   b. Each found it essential in the process to develop confidence among persons.

   c. Each sought to expand the area of choice among leaders, with challenging new ideas, and providing technical information previously unavailable in the community.

4. *Each consultant felt his personal participation was basic to the action process.*

   a. Each cooperated in planning major action projects with citizens.

   b. Each felt the demonstration of certain values to be important:

      1) Personal acceptance of persons expressing opposing points of view in meetings.

      2) Involvement of persons in democratic decision-making.

5. *After the initial organization of the program, each consultant found it necessary to reduce the amount of time which he would spend working in the community.*

a. Each consultant felt it important to prepare the community for a period of less frequent contact.

b. Each consultant sought to let leaders know that he was available during periods of crisis or need in the action program.

Notes

1. Most of the specialists came from the University, although there were others from as far distant as Chicago and St. Louis.

2. These quotations are taken from a letter to the writer (March 30, 1958) in response to questions sent to the consultant about his work in Chapin.

CHAPTER 3

INFLUENCES AND EFFECTS

What kinds of influence or effects were produced in the communities?

RESEARCH METHOD

Random Samples

In order to obtain a quantitive index of the amount of influence created in the four communities, a random sample was selected from the tax rolls of citizen in each community. Three questions were asked of each of thirty individuals selected at random in each community. "Influence" was defined operationally by the amount of citizen "awareness," "participation," and "attendance." The questions asked were:

1. Were you *aware* of the existence of a community council (or community development program) in the community?

2. Did you *attend* one or more meetings which were held in the name of the community council (or community development program)?

3. Did you actively *participate* in the community council (or community development program) during its time of operation in the community?

In regard to the last question on "participation," if the individual had joined in some action project, had served on a committee, or taken office in the program, it was taken as an affirmative answer. Donating money to the program, or answering questions on surveys of censuses were not counted as participation. If persons had actively engaged in conducting the survey or in raising money for the program, this was considered as participation.

Open Interviews

In addition to the brief interviews with the persons in the random sample, more extended open interviews were held with program leaders and participants in the program. Every effort was made to locate persons resisting or opposing the program and to interview them as well for a fully rounded picture of the effect of the program. A set of questions was asked with regard to the initiation, organization, execution, and maintenance of each program as well as the capacity of the program to arouse the interests of local groups to support it. The questions sought to determine the effect of each program on the social structure of the community. The following is one set of questions asked.[1]

A. *Range of Action*

1. Did the physical, economic, and cultural needs of the community come under serious discussion during the three years of operation under study?

2. Did the program take direct action with regard both to physical and cultural (social) problems in the community?[2]

B. *Sentiment*

1. Did at least ¼ of the adult community (or 200 persons, whichever is least in number) become involved each year in assembly or work projects?

2. Did community leaders feel that town meetings continuously held the interests of those in attendance throughout the period of three years?

C. *Class Structure*

1. Were some members from all major class segments of the community supporting the action program through their attendance at town meetings at the beginning of the program?

2. Were members from these classes attending at the end of the three year period?

D. *Organizations*

1. Did the major organizations of the community support the initiation of the program?

2. Did these organizations feel the action organization (the council or the CDA) essential to the welfare of the community at the end of three years?

E. *Financial Requirements*

1. Was the program able to secure funds for its operation during the three years of its operation in a manner acceptable to major organizations?
2. Did the program leaders find a long-range basis for supporting the program which was sufficient for locally defined needs?

F. *Leadership Requirements*

1. Was some means established whereby new officers might become trained for their new positions?
2. Was some provision made for recognition or honors to be given people who had devoted themselves to the efforts of the program?

G. *External Requirements*

1. Was the action organization formally related to a larger regional or national group which could give it support during its trying or critical periods of maintenance?
2. Did local members participate in any larger organization outside the community which was designed to assist the local program over a period of time?

The Class Structure

In order to obtain a cross-reference index of the class structure for comparative purposes among communities, Warner's occupational scale was reproduced. It was then used in interviews with informants to determine relative class positions of each member of the random sample, program leaders, and participants.[3] For the most part the main outlines of the class structure (the laboring class, professionals, businessmen, the power elite) were clearly evident.

In determining who in each community composed the power elite, four questions were posed to informants: 1) what persons have the largest financial investments in the community? 2) who has the greatest number of influential ties to economic and political powers outside the community? 3) who bears the heaviest weight in local decision making? 4) of these persons, who has the longest period of residence or family history in the community? In each case, the number arrived at was between five and ten persons. The elite so designated by informants included only the very top of the power structure.

FINDINGS

Random Samples

The table which follows refers to the samples which were taken in each community in which thirty persons were randomly selected.

The percentages which are listed refer only to the random samples. However, if the percentages are multiplied against the adult population, the numbers which result are supported by the information received in each of the case studies, except Jacksonville. The samples indicate the attendance figures for Chapin to be 147 different persons, for Cobden, 431, for Eldorado, 1,343. With regard to the number of different participants, the figures for Chapin are 41, for Cobden 151, for Eldorado, 929 persons.[4]

It should be noted that the three criteria of "influence" in Table I have some internal consistency inasmuch as they each indicate similar comparisons with other communities. That is, there is no case where one of the measures (percentage of

Table I

RANDOM SAMPLES OF INFLUENCE AMONG ADULTS OVER 21 YEARS

Influence	Communities			
	Chapin (409)	Jacksonville (14,721)	Eldorado (2,785)	Cobden (757)
1. Awareness (Yes)	80%	20%	100%	100%
2. Attendance (Yes)	36%	3%	67%	57%
3. Participation (Yes)	10%	3%	33%	20%

participation, awareness, and attendance) appears inconsistent with its companion criteria in comparison with another community.

Open Interviews

The following table contains the findings to the questions directed at determining the *kinds* of influence created through the action program. The officials of the action organizations were interviewed and found to be in substantial agreement on the answers to each question. Interviews were made in the years 1957-58 and the comparative analysis is made only for the first three years of operation for each program. Since Cobden was in its third year in 1958, it became necessary to hold constant the time span for all the programs when raising questions about their comparative operations.

There were four points which were equally true in all four cases.

1. All action programs obtained the support and attendance of members from major organizations in the community at the initiation of the program.

2. All action programs were attended by persons representing major social class segments of the community at the initiation of the program.

3. All action programs provided short term funds for the action organization.

4. No community developed a long-range financial program to support the action organization.

The remaining hypotheses were answered affirmatively in some communities and negatively in others. In both Eldorado and Cobden, town meeting discussion ranged through the physical, economic, and cultural phases of community development; neither Jacksonville nor Chapin ranged as extensively in their discussion. Both failed to give serious consideration to the economic phases of the community. However, Chapin did take action both in the physical and in the cultural dimensions of the

Table II

COMPARATIVE CONDITIONS OF INFLUENCE

Subject and Question	Communities			
	Chapin	Jacksonville	Eldorado	Cobden
RANGE				
1. Full range in discussion?	No	No	Yes	Yes
2. Full range in action?	Yes	No	Yes	Yes
SENTIMENT				
1. Periodic involvement?	No	No	Yes	No
2. Worthwhile meetings?	No	Yes	No	No
SOCIAL STRUCTURE				
Class Representation				
1. At initiation?	Yes	Yes	Yes	Yes
2. End of three years?	No	No	Yes	No
ORGANIZATIONAL SUPPORT				
1. At initiation?	Yes	Yes	Yes	Yes
2. End of three years?	No	No	Yes	No
MAINTENANCE				
Financial				
1. Short-term funds?	Yes	No	Yes	Yes
2. Long-term basis?	No	No	No	No
Leadership				
1. Training program?	Yes	No	Yes	No
2. Formal honors?	No	No	Yes	No
External Association				
1. External membership?	No	No	Yes	Yes
2. External participation?	No	No	Yes	Yes
Total number of "Yes"	5	3	12	7

community. Only Eldorado periodically involved two hundred persons or more each year in assemblies or work projects within the framework of the action program. Only Jacksonville was able to maintain worth-while meetings consistently over the full period of its existence. "Worth-whileness" of meetings was operationally defined as local program leaders saw it. It should be noted that Jacksonville's meetings were infrequent and each of the other three action organizations had weekly or monthly meetings which lasted over a longer period of time.[5] Only Eldorado evidenced support from organizations and members of all class levels at the end of the three-year period of study. Only Jacksonville was *unable* to maintain funds sufficient for the period of its operation. The term "sufficient" was operationalized in the following question: "Did you (the executive officers of the action organization) feel that lack of funds seriously impeded the successful operation of the program?" In this case, the council's problem was a "lack of funds" to hire persons who would have the time which volunteer leaders did not have. In Chapin and Eldorado a leadership training program was provided by the consulting agency in cooperation with the local action organization. The training program in Chapin was proposed to develop leadership skills but its emphasis was on the development of recreational interests. The Chapin training program came in the second year of the council's existence; the Eldorado program came at the end of the third year of operation. In the beginning of the Eldorado community development program, formal honors were presented to "citizens of the month"—persons who were said locally to have devoted themselves to the "Operation Bootstrap." Only in Eldorado and Cobden were significant and lasting relationships established outside the pattern of the consultant-community relationships. In Eldorado, two regional associations developed in which local citizens participated. One was the Saline Valley Development Association; the other was a regional advisory board. The purpose of the board was to combine the efforts and ideas of all the communities with which the Department of Community Development was consulting, for the purpose of furthering the development of the southern Illinois region.

The implications of these conclusions and the others summarized in Table II will be discussed in later chapters.

Additional Findings

The following generalizations were made after a review of the facts existing in each community action program.

1. The extent of public activity in the action programs was closely associated with the frequency of consultant contact with citizens: i.e., the more frequent the contact, the more public activity; the less frequent, the less activity.

2. During periods of public interest in the program, the action organization served as a symbolic medium through which citizens could make projects legitimate for action in the community.[6]

3. In each case, early town meetings attracted persons who had not been active in civic affairs prior to the initiation of the program.

4. At the end of four years of operation public attendance at town meetings had declined so considerably in each case, that they were discontinued; in three cases, it was decided to call meetings only for special events.

5. After two years of operation the composition of members attending meetings could no longer be considered proportionate to the class levels of the community.[7]

6. After a year of program operation, the active participants were described locally as persons who were also active in other civic organizations.

7. In no case did open organized opposition arise against the action program.

8. In each case, resistance arose among people in some groups in the form of indifference and/or criticism.

9. Each program underwent cycles of public interest and activity.

10. In each case local civic leaders noted that the membership of other voluntary organizations was not increased (or decreased) to any noticeable extent in the wake of the action program in the community.

11. In each case, the action program was something new and exciting for people to talk about, which program leaders admitted broke the deadening routines of community life and opened possibilities for new ideas for the community.

12. New patterns of social relationships were created (in many instances new friendships made) through which new lines of communication were developed with the commonly held interest in "what can be done to better the community?"[8]

13. In each community the action organization provided a new "democratic structure" through which citizens participated.

    a. Prior to the program in each community, there were no town meetings held periodically in which citizens from different walks of life had an equal opportunity to express their views.

    b. Prior to the program in each community, there were no organizations devoted to the interests of the whole community in which membership and participation could be obtained regardless of age, sex, or creed of individual citizens.

NOTES

1. It was assumed that those communities with the most affirmative answers would have experienced the greatest influence. This measure should compare favorably with the quantitative measure found through the random samples.

2. "Physical" needs included such matters as sewage and water systems, street repair, etc.; "economic" needs included a consideration of business or industrial needs; "cultural" needs included such concerns as education, government, recreation, etc.

3. W. Lloyd Warner; Marchia Meeker; Kenneth Eells, *Social Class in America*, Science Research Associates, 1949.

4. In his study of the organization of a health survey under the auspices of a community council, Hunter found that "out of a population of 41,000 in the Salem community, a total of little more than 200 persons, to use a liberal figure, was engaged in the activities of study and action in relation to community-wide problems in health." Floyd Hunter, *Community Organization: Action and Inaction*, (Chapel Hill: University of North Carolina Press, 1956), p. 235.

5. However important maintaining "worth-while meetings" may

be in the views of participants, it was not a sufficient force in itself to combine productively with other factors to create a large measure of influence.

6. In a study of a community health survey, this point is developed: "The role of the Community Council, as a representative body, was to give symbolic approval to the project." Hunter, *op. cit.*, p. 216.

7. This statement is based upon local descriptions of the composition of town meetings.

8. In a recent study of a survey conducted by a community health council, the authors found that "while the formal organizations of the survey committees and the Health Council were no longer in existence, a new social organization had developed, seemingly as a residue, as an unintended creation of the now defunct parent organizations." In pursuing the consequences of this informal network of social relationships, the authors found that new channels of communication had now been created so that action could effectively take place even without the existence of the Health Council. Sower, Holland, Tiedke, Freeman, *Community Involvement*, The Free Press, 1957, p. 276.

CHAPTER 4

DETERMINANTS

What were determinants of the influence created in the communities?

The purpose of this analysis of the case studies is to discover what factors were most basic in creating the different influences in the communities. Only those factors which appeared to have some degree of independence from one another should warrant attention.

These factors were found to be the following: (1) the *external system*, which is divided into four factor components: (*a.*) the ideal model, (*b.*) the consulting agency, (*c.*) the consultant role, (*d.*) status contacts, and (2) the *internal system*, which is divided into three components: (*a.*) the size of the community, (*b.*) the socio-economic structure, and (*c.*) community crisis.

THE EXTERNAL SYSTEM

The Ideal Model

Assuming that the major requirements of the ideal models are followed in practice, the model appears to be more important as a determinant of influence than any other external component. Each model contained different imperatives to act and created different social expectations among leaders.

In Jacksonville, when leaders saw forty people responding for the first town meeting, it was happily received as a positive sign that the "community" was behind the idea. That is, leaders felt that forty organizations were actually participating through their representative officials. In Eldorado, if only three hundred people were attending initial meetings, it was a great disappointment, and leaders wondered where they were falling down on the job. The self-study model in this case called for every able citizen to attend and the only limitation placed on numbers was the size of the auditorium. The measurement of a successful attendance became "standing room only."

Therefore it can be said that the ideal model was more important as a factor producing attendance than the consultant's role, for regardless of what role the consultant might take (within professional expectations), the model would direct his action toward "significant representation" (community council model) or "total participation" (self-study model). Furthermore, the self-study model called for making a census of the community; this was a procedure responsible for creating one hundred per cent awareness of the action program in the community.

Guided by the prerequisites of the council model, the community sought to *coordinate existing resources* through social agencies, and increase leadership effectiveness through more suitable communication. Consultants avoided the idea of creating new organizations in a community already "over-organized," and went to some length to make clear that the council was not "just another organization." On the other hand, the self-study model guided consultants to *create resources*, and to organize *new agencies* to meet needs. Citizens sought to penetrate the community with consultant help, bringing to the surface new talents, ideas, powers, associations, whatever seemed necessary to community development. Consultants looked favorably toward bringing forth leaders into social prominence who previously had not had the interest or the status. In effect, the council model guided consultants to approach the community from top organizational leadership down; the self-study model guided consultants to approach the community as a whole and in depth.[1]

The Consulting Agency

In describing the ideal models earlier, it was noted that the structure and philosophy of the consulting agency would likely be an important determinant of influence. This proved to be true. The agency involved in the council approach had a two-fold purpose: (1) to educate students in human relations and citizenship and (2) to cooperate with communities as they sought to improve local conditions. The assumption underlying the program was that constructive community work could be initiated if the college took an interest in the welfare of the communities in its region. The college agency in this case placed a greater amount of responsibility for self-development and later self-recovery upon the community than did the university agency. While it is clear now that the forces which developed inside each case community were not strong enough to last in the organizational form in which action originated, it is also clear that the major assumption underlying the program was valid—constructive work was begun and communities did accomplish projects which improved conditions.

The assumption underlying the university self-study approach was that the well-being of the communities in the region was of paramount interest to the university, and part of its purpose in existing was to serve them by maximizing their adult education resources to lift the quality of living for people in the area. Consultants there did not have dual roles (teacher and consultant); they gave full time to consultation in the communities.

In Cobden, the time spent in the first two years for the action program was estimated at 2,363 hours. The consultant's time in Eldorado was not estimated but there is substantial reason to believe more time was spent there. Consultant time in Chapin in the first two years was estimated at 108 hours, and in Jacksonville at 242 hours. No daily record was kept of consultant time. The figure is only the consultant's estimate based on recalling from memory the hours or days he spent each month in the community. Without a more accurate record available the differences between the two latter cases were too small to be considered significant. However, between the two regions it seems quite clear that the amount of consultant time spent in the community was closely related to the amount of influence and community activity which was measured in the random samples.

Consultant Role

The consultant role is understood as that pattern of relationships which is created by the agency representative in placing the ideal model into operation with the cooperation of local citizens. Although the limits placed on the consulting time by an agency does strongly affect the extent of influence or activity in the community, it does not determine the pattern of relationships which the consultant may come to develop because of his own orientation and background. The case studies give evidence that the unique differences in consultant approaches served as an independent variable.

At the beginning of the study it seemed altogether reasonable to predict that "the greater the size of the community, the less amount of influence would be created in proportion to that size." However, two of the studies invalidated this hypothesis. In Eldorado, a town of 4,000, there was more attendance and participation recorded in proportion to its size than in Cobden, a town of 1,000. The ideal model and the agency remained constant as variables of influence, but the role of the consultant was different. The differential influence can only have been due to a difference in the consulting approach (involving a configuration of interests, skills, values) which was brought to the community scene.

Status Contacts

The reference made to "status contacts" involves those agencies and personalities which represent outside prestige and power to the community. The case studies demonstrate that certain types of outside contact and communication are cause for considerable social change. In several instances external agencies were largely responsible for the creation of a deeper sense of community and a greater collective participation in certain events in the programs.

The most dramatic occurrence was the television show in Eldorado. The expectation of being in a national spotlight virtually electrified the community. It went far to solidify gains made in the program up to that point. The timing of the event, to be sure, cannot be underestimated for its importance in creating the effect. It came at the culmination of the self-study phase and signaled the transition into action. A later filming of the Eldorado story, following this episode, did not have any comparable effect.

There were other outside factors operating on the programs which could easily be overlooked, yet are highly significant. There was first, of course, the outside consulting agency helping to initiate and guide the program. Secondly, outside news media carried weight because of their status. There were news articles about the self-study communities in large metropolitan dailies; the local action stories were printed in nationally distributed magazines. Thirdly, there was contact with well-known professional people in fields of specialization.

These different types of outside contacts all carried some prestige in the minds of local citizens and provided an authoritative image from which the value of local action could be judged. Furthermore, these contacts were primarily interested in giving recognition to the community for what they were seeking to accomplish.

The function of these outside contacts was to place emphasis upon the people in town being one undivided group. This lessened the chance for individual differences to become so important as to destroy the unity necessary to the program. The town was, as one person said, an "organic living whole," which acted and lived as one. It might be assumed that the more outside agencies referred to the town as one unit in everything it accomplished, the more people came to accept the reference as the controlling or guiding image in all that they did.

The symbolic character of the relationships developed were in some instances patriarchal in form. For example, the television program in Eldorado represented the nation, symbolically perhaps a great father figure to the community. The consultants too were subject to a similar projection as they sought to praise, blame, or challenge the community regarding its actions. An analogy found to be fitting in the news accounts of the self-study programs was that of a doctor-patient relationship in which the patient (the community) receives prescriptions from the doctor (consultant) during the time that it took for the community to become healthy again. Undoubtedly there is some truth in such analogies, but they are not adequate in themselves to describe the relationships that unfolded. Diagnosis and prescription were not the only, nor the most important functions expressed in the relationship of consultant to community, and the agency-community relationship continued in many cases during the "healthy" periods of development. Eventually it may be said the consulting agency comes to be helped by the community as it improves the conditions of the region of which they are both a part.

THE INTERNAL SYSTEM

Size of Community

There were clear differences in influence created in the two communities which contrasted so extremely in size (Chapin and Jacksonville) even though the same ideal model and consulting agency were involved and the consultant roles were similar. Many of the differences can best be explained on the basis of size alone and the accompanying differences in social organization.

The Chapin town meetings were more informal (mainly because they were smaller) and the council moved more quickly and easily on a variety of community projects. Decision-making in the larger Jacksonville council was slower and "action" tended to be directed toward making a survey or gathering facts about resources rather than direct treatment of problems, as in Chapin. The Jacksonville council felt it more important to retain the participation of official delegates, while the Chapin council came to accept an informal nucleus of leaders regardless of their official capacity. The sheer size and complexity of social organization in the larger city seemed to predestine the council to move more slowly and deliberately as a means of convincing the multi-interest membership of the importance of certain problems.

In their efforts to communicate with a hundred representa-

tives, Jacksonville leaders had to use mass media methods, much
different from those of Chapin where leaders sought to communicate with twelve to twenty members. While the Jacksonville
council found it possible to function much as the proposed ideal
model (a "federation," a "clearinghouse"), the Chapin council
functioned more as a community club (minus the emphasis on
entertainment usually present in such groups) and was more
open to separate individuals' concerns. It is concluded that
differences in size affected the role which the council organization took in these two communities.

Socio-Economic Classes

The most distinctive conclusion that can be drawn from an
analysis of the socio-economic classes is that their type of involvement was similar in all cases. This was particularly surprising in
view of the fact that each of the four communities differed so
greatly in type, and that different models were brought into
play in the four cases. The character of the community class
structure appears to be heavily dependent upon the national
socio-economic organization. The local community action programs, while affecting it, did not change it to any significant
degree.

In each action program, steady active support of the program
activities was found in the *upper status groups*. The seven-point
system which was used to estimate the relative positions of
persons in the four communities supported this conclusion. In
other words, although a professional group proved to be a source
of leadership in Jacksonville and business leaders were the steady
strength in Eldorado, in both, the leaders were rated as "two"
and "three" according to the occupational scale which guided
the estimates of local informants.

The role which the local *power elite* came to have in the
action programs is in some ways surprising. In each case the
elite gave some initial support to the program (although in
Eldorado there were mixed feelings); they never actually offici-
ated in the action organization itself. The power figures in
Eldorado and Cobden did develop interest in the economic

groups organized (i.e., Chambers of Commerce, industrial foundations). The fact was, however, that the action group itself (the community council, or CDA) in each case did not develop into a crucial permanent group in the community. The interests of the power figures remained aligned with those associations created to develop the community economically. Although leadership among the power elite was of a non-public character, it can be concluded that the smaller the size of the community the more public or socially visible their leadership became.

In each case the participation and interest of the *working class* lessened with time. The decrease in interest may have been due to the fact that the process of community action requires greater adjustments for the laborer than for others in differing occupational segments of the community. The gathering of data and fact-finding, the objective analysis of it, the long-range planning, budgeting, etc., are less a part of his daily life and occupational activities than of those of other groups in the community. In view of the value orientation of the average laborer, it is remarkable that his interest was retained as long as it was in Eldorado. In the other communities his interest did not last much longer than the initial meetings. In Eldorado the basis of continued interest was the hope of obtaining immediate returns on industry and perhaps, secondly, on the immediate social pleasures and novelty which the program created in community life. Without disregarding the importance of other phases of programming, the value of personal enjoyment and immediate rewards from community action cannot be underestimated in assessing the outcome of class involvement.

As a rule, the proportion of persons from each class participating in the action program was not in the same proportion as in the community as a whole. The Warner studies would suggest that the largest proportion of the community is at the "common man" level and below, but the largest proportions of active participants in all programs was above this level. Even at the initiation of the programs, when all social levels were reported as "represented," the truth was they were not represented proportionally. Only in Eldorado during the self-study phase might it be suggested that the class interests were proportioned with some comparability to the real proportions in the town. When this occurred, the working man had some measure of control over the program, and highest status persons in the community were proportionally in the minority. This condition was highly unusual and short-lived.

The nature of the class system and the nature of the action program seemed to contain polar interests, one seeking to divide the community, the other to unify it. It may be said that both functioned to effect some kind of stability in social organization, but they did not coincide at every point, and together they tended to threaten stability. The philosophy of the action programs emphasizes democratic equality; the class system inherently emphasizes inequality. A persisting state of tension was written into their coexistence.[2] In two communities there were clear indications that the status of a number of *individuals* in the community was raised through leadership; but the main class structure continued unchanged. Although the precise effect the program had on the class structure was not a matter of measurement or design in this study, it may be concluded that the existing class system was an important determinant of the way in which the action program became a part of the community life.

The Community Crisis

The studies seem to give some insight into the role which a "crisis" may come to play in a program, and they clarified several points for future research which were not altogether clear prior to this investigation.

It has often been assumed that a crisis is a valuable starting point for community action because it prepares people to make great social changes. A closer look at its role, however, indicates that it may function to restrict the operation of the program and limit its chances of success. In a positive sense, it creates great potential for change, but at the same time it produces conditions unfavorable to community action.[3] It becomes apparent that the concept cannot be wholly sufficient as an objective variable distinguishing why one action program had more influence than another. It must be analyzed into subtypes, such as political, social, or economic crisis, which may have more direct significance as a functional or dysfunctional element in the operation of a community program. Furthermore, two other types must be distinguished: first, an objective condition of the internal system, and second, the more subjective "definition of the situation."[4] The same internal conditions may exist in two communities, yet the leaders in one community may define it as a crisis, and the leaders in the other may not.

The concept of crisis may become an integral part of the ideal model and be applied to any community regardless of its condition. A crisis touches upon the survival energies of participants and provides a deeper source of motivation toward collective action than the process of calling upon latest interests for community improvement. In short, the concept of crisis may be both a reflection of the unique internal condition of the community and a part of the philosophy of action underlying the framework of the ideal model.

Notes

1. Murray Ross has distinguished action approaches according to their objectives which is suggestive of the differences discovered here. Murray Ross, *Case Histories in Community Organization*, (New York: Harper & Brothers, 1958), p. 16.

2. The polar problem of community sentiment and social stratification is originally discussed in Robert M. McIver's *Society*, (New York: Rinehart and Co., Inc., 1949), pp. 358, 359.

3. See the chapter titled "Community Development Process: A Case Study" for a more complete description of this role as the consultant and local leaders saw it in one community.

4. W. I. Thomas' original formulation of this concept is appropriate here: "Preliminary to any self-determined act of behavior there is always a stage of examination and deliberation which we may call 'definition of the situation.' And actually not only concrete acts are dependent on the definition of the situation, but gradually a whole life-policy and the personality of the individual himself follow from a series of such definitions." (W. I. Thomas, *The Unadjusted Girl*, Boston: Little, Brown and Company, 1923, p. 41.)

CHAPTER 5

PROBLEMS AND POSSIBILITIES

Why didn't the ideal models work entirely
as expected?

PROBLEMS IN STRUCTURE AND CONCEPTION

Various problems arose as the ideal models were placed into operation. Program leaders tended to blame problems and failures on particular individuals in each program (i.e., leaders did not have the skill, or were not very well-liked, or didn't have the time to devote to it, etc.). However, a careful analysis reveals that there were actually certain structural problems not visible to local citizens—mostly arising from misconceptions or gaps in the descriptions of the ideal models—which went beyond a normal leader's capacity to resolve them. The examination of these areas would be of great aid in helping to frame more adequate models for future use in community development. The following problem areas which became apparent will be considered: misconceptions of council role, general misconceptions of model, lack of continuation of the programs, and additional problems in structure.

Council Role

There appeared to be confusion and differences of opinion among local leaders regarding the role of the community council in three of the case communities. Three major points of confusion may be noted:

First, the model did not sufficiently clarify the role of the council in taking action on problems itself, independently of its many constituent organizations. Taking any effective action often meant running counter to the vested interests of one or more of its represented groups. The democratic procedures for handling such an internal problem were never specified for local guidance in the formal model.

Second, there was confusion as to whether or not the council was justified in taking action upon industrial and physical problems; customarily these are within the province of the chamber of commerce and the city council. The tendency existed for consultants to define the primary interest as being "welfare" and to consider other problems only if they created some adverse effect upon social welfare. However, it was found that the smaller the community the more likely the industrial and physical problems came to be defined as legitimate for the council to tackle directly.

Third, the model described the council as a "clearinghouse" which could coordinate specialized services, a "federation" of organizations which could surmount the problems of overlapping or competitive interests. No such function was realizable or even necessary in the smaller communities where everyone knew fairly well what other groups were doing and there were no professional agencies. The models failed to take into account differences in size among communities and the necessity of the action organization to adapt itself accordingly.

General Misconceptions of Model

Certain misconceptions about the nature of social action arose from gaps in both models, but especially in the community council approach. For example, consultants and local leaders assumed in many cases that formal notices of community meetings (via newspaper publicity and postcards to delegates) would be enough to stimulate representatives to attend meetings. This in itself did not prove sufficient. Similarly it was assumed that factual publicity about community problems (e.g., so many houses do not have running water, toilets, etc.) would be an adequate medium for reaching people personally. That is, contact through mass media was assumed to be effective without organizing direct, personal contact among people concerned.

The rational emphasis in the council model brought about no real appreciation of the necessities for creating sentiment as a basis for community action. In contrast, the self-study approach emphasized persuasive methods to a maximum, including slogans, formal ceremonies of dedication, symbols of community, and bringing people together in purpose and unity. Assuming that the council model was directed toward professional interests and was not designed for rallying large numbers of people behind its causes, it nevertheless did not give importance to the nonrational elements of community life. The importance of sentiment in community action cannot be denied; the degree to which it must be emphasized in particular community programs has yet to be more fully examined.

Lack of Continuation

In no case did the action organization—the council or the CDA—continue to function regularly and effectively after the fourth year. Rather than simply attribute such a common phenomenon to failure of particular leaders in each case, it seems more accurate to diagnose it as a structural problem. There appear at least two basic reasons for the failure to continue, reasons which may be attributed to the functions of the organization in the community and in the larger society.

First, after the consultant had reduced the frequency of his visits to the community there was no larger regional or national body outside the community which was organized to furnish support to the local action group when it confronted difficulties. The consulting agency acted in this capacity for the first few years, but inevitably the contact was reduced or withdrawn entirely. In contrast, for instance, a Kiwanis or Rotary Club maintains this external tie. A national organization supports the local group through periodicals, national purpose, intercommunity movements of members, a national hierarchy of officers, and sometimes financial support and counseling services during time of organizational crisis. In the case of community councils, admittedly there does exist a national organization of community chests and councils, but in neither case under study did the councils find the relationship one they could develop for their purposes. The national council is closely associated with the chest movement and is not designed to be related to councils at the local level as fraternal agencies, lodges, churches, or as other groups in the community are related.

Second, in no case was any permanent fund-raising foundation for the council or the CDA established. The self-study approach emphasized spontaneous fund raising, but offered no other alternative when this became insufficient. The community council model purposely avoided the idea of fund-raising techniques, and suggested obtaining money from the community chest. The case study in Jacksonville revealed extreme reluctance on the part of some council leaders to accept chest money, for fear that organizations would feel obligated to contribute to the chest. It was suggested that all organizations contribute some amount independently to the council; but a number of groups were state agencies and were prohibited from joining on such a basis.

Additional Problems of Structure

The council model called for total representation of major community groups, yet in the larger community, complexities existed which ultimately led to the dissolution of the organization. Three structural problems in particular stand out.

First, the work in maintaining an up-to-date file on so many groups (in Jacksonville, eighty-odd groups), the detailed procedure in obtaining sanction to join, contacting members of meetings, etc., were altogether too much for voluntary efforts of citizens to continue very long.

Second, the diversity of group interest among delegates (the real estate board, the Negro American Legion, the white Legion, the women's club, the YMCA, etc.) made it next to impossible to develop a project of vital interest to all, so that interest in attending meetings soon waned even though meetings were conducted in a satisfactory manner. Assigning delegates to special interest committees met with apathy, since it tended to put formal structure before personal interest.

Third, a cause of apathy can also be found in some arbitrary appointments made by club or agency presidents. Delegates without motivational support were assigned to attend council meetings. On the other hand, where some strong interest developed in the council, a division of loyalty would often arise between the two groups (membership group *vs.* council), with the vector between these two forces again producing apathy.

ALTERNATIVES IN COUNCIL STRUCTURE

Lacking a paid staff from established agencies in the community, it is clear that a "permanent" action group *will not last long*. If it does survive, it may become an exclusive club not recognized as representative of the community, in which case it loses its original purpose and identity. There are various alternative approaches, nevertheless, which are reasonable to consider in fulfilling the objectives of council structures.

One approach to creating an effective council would be to set a time limit on it and then focus on special problems. That is, critical community problems do arise which arouse multi-organizational interest and demand attention. Councils can be, and have been, organized for this purpose. When the problems are no longer critical or when they have been solved, the council rests its case and disbands. The council structure serves its purpose in time of need.

Another approach would involve a permanent council with the purpose of creating annual or periodic community conferences to discuss community problems and needs, but serving in no action capacity. That is, a representative council or committee would plan for delegates to attend a day-long (or weekend) conference which would function to supply new ideas, inform each organization of what the others are doing, and review new methods for solving local problems. The meetings would exist only as a medium of exchange. There would exist no formal structure except that necessary to organize the meetings at regular intervals.

Neither of the above-mentioned approaches would be likely to meet the ideals inherent in current approaches to community development. An active permanent association, representative of the community, is conceivable, but would require considerable educational effort to bring it about on a permanent basis. To meet the problems existing in the case studies, a third approach must be considered. An executive council might be financially supported by and elected from the three major divisions of community organization: the city council (physical needs); the chamber of commerce (economic needs); and the chest or voluntary groups (welfare needs). Such a structure would require new model definitions, *but might contain a greater potential for modern planning in community development than any of the previously conceived models of permanent action groups.* The position of such a group in the community requires further study.

FUNCTIONAL REQUIREMENTS

On the basis of the case-study analysis, for any association to survive in effective operation in the community, certain functional requirements must be met. These requirements, in summary-outline form, are described below.

1. *Community Sentiment,* sustained by:

   a) Periodic common activities in which considerable proportions of the community participate.

   b) Symbols which identify and distinguish the association's position in community life.

   c) Frequent interaction within the leadership nucleus.

2. *Set of Beliefs,* consisting of:

   a) Values reinforcing (or compatible with) basic traditions or the general culture.

   b) Objectives which are a reflection of locally felt needs.

3. *Program of Action,* which:

   a) Gives adequate recognition to contributions made by leaders from differing social divisions in the community.

   b) Provides visible achievements made possible by the development association to which people may refer.

4. *Program of Planning*, which:

   a) Seeks to anticipate future developments in the community and to prepare for them.

   b) Provides a full range of study covering both the physical and the cultural phases of community development.

5. *Community Support*, through:

   a) Financial contributions from major segments of the community.

   b) Official representation of the major interests of the community.

6. *Institutionalization*, creating:

   a) Established procedures for meeting recurring needs in a way which contains instrumental as well as end satisfactions for participants.

   b) Programs which are supported by established institutions of the general culture.

7. *An External system*, which:

   a) Reveals interest in how the community takes action *as* a community, and sets forth ideas as well as ideals with which local citizens can work.

   b) Interacts with participants on the local scene.

CHAPTER 6

THE COMMUNITY DEVELOPMENT PROCESS: A CASE STUDY

How does a community undergo radical social change guided by an outside agency?

FIELD DESCRIPTION

Introduction

The Eldorado community is selected for special study because the changes there took place more rapidly and radically than in the other cases. The program provides an unusual opportunity for students of socio-cultural change to examine the elements which contribute toward making such a transition. This field study is made from the perspective of the change agents themselves on the basis of interviews with them.

The purpose of this analysis is to reflect the social meanings underlying the outward changes and achievements of the program. It is not the purpose to promote any part of the process as right or wrong. It is the purpose to understand the process of change as it took place in the personal lives and personal outlooks of the participants. The interpretation begins with the personal diagnosis of the consultant which later came to be accepted by community leaders and then moves on to describe what appeared in this case to be the major phases of the change process.

The Consultant's Diagnosis of Conditions

Some outsiders have said that Eldorado was in a state of crisis; social breakdown had occurred, and this condition was more important in creating change than was any proposed "process."

This image can be misleading, for local participants and the consultant would state that it misapprehends the true character of the situation, and overlooks a major portion of the consultant's (and the leaders') responsibility to the process. It is true that channels of communication and cooperation were to a large extent broken down, and were not functioning in a manner one would expect from a normal community. But it is also true that other social forms and cultural patterns had taken their place.

There were factional jealousies and serious organizational rivalries; there were long-nourished hurts and animosities and divisive stereotyping which were making it impossible for people to work together on a community level. Many of these differences which were crippling community organization were known locally to have a long history, covering generations of family life. And these differences were heightened in their intensity through the economic plight that spread throughout the community in the form of a general hopelessness.

It is true that the situation may have presented a great energetic potential underneath this divisive social pattern, but the consultant saw that the problem of community development would be made more difficult by this fact. After he had time to survey the whole state of affairs, he told community leaders that quite frankly the town would have to be "dynamited" before anything could get moving. This statement had purpose and meaning to the people of Eldorado. "Dynamiting" and "blasting" the community were terms familiar to a coal mining town, and it was at this point that a positive response was initiated, particularly among the laboring men of the community. The consultant, accepting something of the local culture as his own, began at a level in which the community was existing and then moved from there, working to open up new social patterns and even to establish a new language to explain the process of community development.

The consultant saw that a major portion of his time would need to be directed toward creating a climate wherein people could come to *believe* in themselves and their fellow citizens, and ultimately in the whole process of community development. The methodological problem consisted primarily of producing situations in which people would have the will to believe, where they would have the incentive to move ahead, where they would "want what they ought to want"; when this was done, the problem became one of helping them to achieve what they wanted, to actually acquire and possess this new way of living together in a community. In other words, a breakdown of the old patterns and an emergence of the new patterns centered on the problem of creating a belief in people's capacity to work out a solution to their problems, and then providing the method by which it could be done. The "method" came first in the form of an idea, a concept.

A New Concept is Introduced

The process began at a point when there was a measure of dissatisfaction, or more important, a sign of interest to engage in something new. The stage in which the consultant entered the picture was at the point where people were seeking to locate and define a   commonly felt problem. The consultant played an important role in helping define just what the problem really was and how to locate it in the community.

Locating and Defining the Problem: Challenge and Response

In the process of defining the problem, the consultant explained the new concept. In the case of Eldorado there was a difference in the community's definition of their problem and the consultant's definition. The community saw their problem as a lack of industry. The consultant saw this as an important aspect of a much larger problem. Although lifelong residents felt they knew their community quite well, the consultant boldly suggested that there might be a great many things which they did not know that were important in helping them solve their problem. Local people were concerned about their problem; the consultant wondered if they were really concerned about their problem *enough* to deal with its real source, a complete lack of "community." In the consultant's statement of the problem, there was a hidden challenge. The definition did not solely consist of a rational analysis of what was needed in the community or what steps were necessary in the plan of action; it began with a demonstration of the process itself, a challenge to act.

In the meeting of the delegation from the community with the consultant (and later in town meetings) the whole plan of operation was objectively discussed and considered. The important point to note, however, is the process by which this was done. The model was set forth in such a way as to make it desirable, yet capable of being questioned and discussed with regard to making a decision. The community had to decide for themselves whether or not to choose this path. The consultant said it was their decision, and he could work with them *only under these conditions.* A new relationship was being established. The will of the community[1] was being deeply respected (and perhaps tapped for the first time in many years) and a decision was made. At the same time the decision placed full responsibility for the direction of the program in the hands of the consultant, since he was now the accepted authority on the model for action. The consultant, in turn, made it very clear that full responsibility for the implementation of the model was in the hands of the community. The relationship this produced was almost patriarchal in form, but something new had been added. The relationship had been ushered in by the will of the community, and could be terminated at the discretion of their leaders. This was a period of transition; it was a period of learning, a period of new birth, in which the consultant was to serve as midwife.

Both before and after the decision to proceed had been made, the consultant felt it his responsibility to prepare the community (through conversations with a core of community leaders, and through town meeting speeches) for the ordeal which they were about to encounter. A state of readiness had to be created wherein people would be prepared for hard work and plenty of leadership, and at the same time be capable of looking forward to the process with a fair degree of optimism. The public conception of community responsibility for the kind of program which was about to take place was fundamental to getting the process under way. This was a new approach, and its possibilities were exciting.

Tension and New Meaning

Tension developed as a natural part of the new situations which were created. A delegation makes a visit to the university for the first time; a whole community engages the services of a university to help work out its problems; a committee chairman finds himself forced into a position where he must speak out before a formal gathering—all this produces tension, and this tension served as the instrument of change. It is difficult to follow in the traditional grooves and say, "It won't work," when everyone is beginning to realize they have never tried such a method before. The uneasiness and expectation diffused among leaders acted as the cutting edge on the cords of old resistance.

As the operation on the old patterns began and the "surgery" was about to commence, the whole concept was beginning to slumber under an anaesthetic of its own making. Unconsciously people were not only beginning to dream of the future, but of the past. They sought to find a relationship between this new outer experience and past generations, with their traditions, their religion, the philosophy around which they had built their lives. And there was a discovery which was simple but difficult for the outsider to understand; however, it was highly meaningful to individuals participating in the process. It was the discovery that these ideas were not really new at all, but old ideas in new form. Some suddenly recognized that this was really the basis of religion, although it was not stated in biblical language. Some recognized the meaning of democracy, seemingly for the first time. The pure experience of decision-making and responsibility for the direction of community life became a reality. It was as though suddenly a fresh wind lifted a fog which had settled over old forgotten values, and a new light was cast upon them. With the new understanding could come a change in one's whole life orientation.[2]

The more personally involved people become, the greater potential for change, and the more urgency is given to public acceptance of the new idea. This need not be thought of as an exclusive experience, rather as an inclusive one, where satisfaction is not obtained until a basis is found where everyone may be included in the process.

The more personally involved people become, the greater change was an important one, and leaders were just beginning to realize it. It was true that people had thought local traditions would be the most difficult patterns to change, but the experience of the leaders indicated that it required another tradition to do it. That is, the pivotal point for change in Eldorado was upon another deeper, more inviolable set of values which proved to be the foundation of the new social pattern.[3]

People wanted to change; they wanted the whole idea to work. The more the possibilities of changing the community were discussed in conferences, on the street, in the home, the more they became conceivable; and the more people's imaginations were freed to operate on ideas which they never before would have thought to entertain.

The Imaginative Process

The imagination of citizens was courted early in the Eldorado program; new ideas, new imagery was creatively stirred through vivid descriptions of what had happened in other communities and what could happen to Eldorado. The movement from an "idea to do something," to the actual doing of it, was seen by the consultant to be a rather slow process, but one to be understood as part of community development. That is, the process by which an idea becomes transformed into a "felt need," becomes shared by leaders in the community, then engages the will of the community, and finally issues forth in action, is one to be carefully nurtured and followed with expectation. For example, although people had begun to think about the idea of renovating the city hall in the early portion of the program, it was five months before it actually was renovated.

The stimulus to working on the city hall as part of the program came from the consultant. In his first visits to the community, he noted its poor condition, and the fact that for Eldorado residents it was a collective symbol representing the entire community. The decision early took hold in his mind to make this one of the ideas around which to build a community project. It was something that had to become significant to local citizens, something that had to be constructed first in the imaginations of the people in the community. If it didn't succeed in taking hold, however, it was "just one of a hundred or more" ideas toward which the consultant and leaders were to concentrate their efforts.

The consultant suggested that the census headquarters should be located in the city hall. This would give people an opportunity to see and feel the deteriorated condition into which their community building had fallen. Hundreds of people went in and out of the hall during the census taking; many had never been in the place before and never obtained a sense of what it was like. In the process of census instruction, the consultant continually pointed out what could happen as a result of this census work. He would drop comments here and there about this and that, about the dirty flag standing over in the corner, the broken floor boards underneath their feet—all simply hypothetical examples of what needed to be done. People began hearing about this problem late in October, 1953, but action did not begin to unfold until after the Beautification Committee met in February, 1954.

While imagination was being stimulated, another phase of the process was emerging simultaneously which spanned the program from beginning to end. New confidence had to be brought within the grasp of people before they could seek those values which they had begun to think about and entertain approvingly.

Developing Confidence

The development of new confidence began early and went through several phases where the community (a) came to the point where they could accept the fact that social change was humanly possible, (b) was given outside recognition and support for making this change, (c) realized the importance of what was happening locally in the light of a larger purpose, (d) made preliminary demonstrations of its workability, (e) could refer to successful demonstrations in the past as a point upon which to build in the future.

Belief in the idea that change was humanly possible in Eldorado was first stimulated through the organization of LAID to do something about employment conditions. But it did not really take firm hold until talks with the consultant began. The fact that the model had worked successfully in other communities first led to the abstract idea that at least it was possible for some communities, and secondly to stimulate thinking about what could be done in Eldorado. At the same time it increased the confidence of people in their consultant, who had been part of the other action programs about which he talked. He spoke with authority. And the assurance and confidence which was part of his own make-up served to bolster their own. It was a beginning, but it was not enough.

The community had to realize that this whole effort was part of a large purpose, and that their participation in furthering this purpose was significant to others outside the community. The purpose was to make democracy real instead of an ideal frustrated by the realities (economic and otherwise) of community living. The purpose was to help strengthen democracy. Where else was democracy to live, if not in the communities of America? Where else should it begin, if not in Eldorado, a town in dire need of it? Outside specialists were brought into town meetings throughout the program to talk with people about what they were doing. There was common interest to be found among the outside "authorities" and the average man of Eldorado: this was an experiment in living. Eldorado people were not only making headlines for what was beginning to happen, but they were doing research on a process of creating a new community. This project would contain errors, but that was because no one in the country knew exactly how a community should go about remaking itself—not even the authorities. When the authorities were there, they were not only there to provide technical knowledge, but to share in the process of discovery. How can communities make democracy work?

"Preliminary demonstrations" of what could be done were essential to developing confidence. People needed to "get the feel" of working together. Only when action actually began to take place can we say that people began to make confidence a definite part of their lives. But these early action efforts in Eldorado were also seen as stages of "preparation" for other efforts to come. To speak accurately, it should be said that this whole phase, including *all* action projects, discussion groups, published reports, etc., constituted *preparation* for times to come. Although there were beginnings and ends to particular projects within the process, people conceived them to be a preparation for the future. The preliminary projects, if they could be called that, became a basis upon which people could build their confidence in going on not only toward more important action projects, but also toward the long-range planning periods which the consultant felt to be just as essential to the process of community development.

Release and Renewal

After leaders and early participants had been given an opportunity to think about the new idea, to work out imaginatively its implications for themselves and the community, to gain some measure of confidence in bringing the idea into reality, a fourth phase appeared in the process of purposive development: release and renewal. It meant letting go of the old way and embracing the new. As the program got underway in Eldorado, leaders were encouraged to break loose and think of anything that was unusual or fantastic for the community. This applied first to dramatizing meetings in order to bring out interest and attendance. (Getting people to meetings meant blowing fire sirens, ringing church bells, flying airplanes over the town, staging parades, etc.) Then it came to apply to opening new ideas and goals for community development. A new value was placed on the nonconformist; the person who could think of the oddest and most stimulating ideas was now favorably recognized, whereas before he would have been thought queer and out of place. Getting people to set new standards meant such things as dreaming up the idea of all merchants getting up early each morning to sweep the street in front of their stores, or organizing an "alley-rally" to clear residential back roads and by-roads of dirt and trash, or drumming up new industry from local talent—all of which grew into reality in Eldorado, out of the "crazy" ideas which people (including the consultant) felt inclined to express. The rigidity of thought patterns, the fear of expressing oneself in a new way, was done away with; created in its place was an atmosphere of acceptance and a sense of enjoyment in the process.

There was a new freedom of expression in early meetings, which was released in songs, clowning skits, and whatever else seemed to create interest. It was hard for some people to accept this, but the multiplicity of changed faces and behaviors began to weaken resistance to this unconventional way of doing things. Leaders took the lead in acting with mischief and fun, and this added to a more general acceptance. With release came a reason for acting this way—it was for the good of the program, if nothing else, a sacrifice for the community. With renewal came new symbols and slogans. "December 7th" was the day selected to launch the study program. People thought of this as the day that a wrong was recognized and a whole nation mobilized to correct it; and so this was the day that war was to be declared on the evils of the Eldorado community. And summing up the whole endeavor was "Operation Bootstrap," a phrase which symbolized the revolution taking place.

Finding and Facing the Facts

The process of finding the facts is a matter of well-established scientific procedure in institutions of Western sociey. However, its more rigorous forms are unknown to large segments of every community; it was a process which did not come easy for Eldorado, for the median level of completed schooling was 8.4 grades. Curiosity about community facts, objectivity in dealing with these facts, and honesty and courage to face these facts, were real problems with which people struggled.

The fact-finding process began with the census and with the the consultant as teacher. One hundred and eighty people were introduced to the formal procedures of gathering facts. Out of this experience a new curiosity was born. As the information began to flow in, people began to wonder and ask themselves: how many deteriorated houses are there in this town; how many don't have inside toilets? As the count of citizens in the community began to be tabulated, each day people were asking, "Will the number go over 1,000? 2,000? 3,000?" People really became interested; notes were placed on the doors of houses by occupants who expected the census-taker, but had to leave: "I'm at Joe's, be back in half an hour." The respondents of this census project (which included everybody) seemed to become just as involved as the leaders themselves.

The process of building a scientific acceptance of the facts was proceeding hand in hand with the breakdown of the old forms of beliefs about the community and the creation of new beliefs. People were facing the facts, and sometimes the facts were publicly embarrassing. The Community Characteristics Survey was an early experience of what amounted to a painful airing of dirty linen. People were shocked to discover their survey revealed that they felt themselves individually seeking to "lead a Christian life," while they felt that their neighbors were seeking "financial success." Later, people admitted it was a buried truth which no one could have told them publicly—except themselves. The evidence was indisputably there; they had made the indictment, there was no one else to blame. The poor quality of many living quarters, the number of outside toilets in the community, were facts they had furnished themselves—facts which began to shake public conceptions of the community. The traditional speeches of politicians seeking re-election, for example, could no longer drone on without the new self-consciousness. Something had to take the place of these old platitudes. Something of value was there. It was a new commitment to the truth, to honesty and objectivity, all made possible because now something could be done about it.

The way of finding facts was a way of telling the truth, and it was becoming possible to be thoroughly honest about everything. Illustrating this phase of the process, one citizen in Eldorado recalled (to the writer) a meeting held among businessmen, in which a very heated discussion took place about whether or not a particular industry should be allowed to locate in Eldorado. Everyone (including the consultant) told the truth about how they felt toward the industry, and even though some sharp and sometimes angry remarks were made in the session, there was time at the end to come to a decision agreeable to everyone. He said the men there "grew" because of that meeting since they came to accept something of each other's views in spite of the strength with which they held to their own.

One of the owners of a medium-sized hardware store in town had been in the thick of community development right from the beginning. A banker who was also one of the owners of a large business in town had not taken active part—at least not as active as people thought he should in view of his highly respected position in the community. The hardware store owner boldly wrote him a letter, frankly stating that this was an important program and of all the people in town, he ought to be involved in it. The letter was bold because in the former state of the community, this was a little man telling a big man what he ought to do for the town. Ordinarily this could have only caused greater alienation, but the sheer truthfulness and good intent revealed in the letter was enough to break down resistance and cause the banker to show the letter to circles of friends as a testimony of what the program was doing. It was an act which brought him into full participation in the program.

People found that the honesty and objectivity which came with self-study extended to other areas of human relations. And they found that it did not conflict with the personal elements so basic to the release of the old patterns and the ushering in of the new way of life.

The Possession of a Belief

The assumption made in the approach to the community of Eldorado we may interpret as this: the definition of the problem, the introduction of a new idea, imagination and rational discussion focused on community improvement, and even the gathering of facts about the community, is not enough to break the traditional barriers of personal prejudice and general apathy, and bring people where they can really possess the treasure of a changed community. People must combine themselves into a new unit, in which everyone may join, young and old, the sick and able, in active demonstration of how the process may work, and work effectively.

Total Involvement in Active Demonstration

Total participation in action meant that everyone who was willing and able joined in contributing something to a new creation in community life. One of the first major demonstrations in Eldorado was the renovation of their city hall; a second major effort was placed toward creating a community park. This was the choice of leaders. They wanted to make the park into something of which everyone could be proud. It was the kind of project toward which every person could contribute, even if they were willing to come to the park construction only to pick up loose paper or to dig a drainage ditch next to the road.

Like the city hall, there were reasons for choosing the park as a likely project around which the community could center its efforts These reasons had come to be learned by local leaders.

1) It had meaning for everyone in the community.
2) It was a project that people could start and finish in a relatively brief period.
3) It was something in which almost everyone in town could participate.
4) It included all phases of community life: carpentry, human relations, recreation, public relations, financing, etc.

Total involvement meant that everything within the community was brought into operation with the project. All trades and professions were seen to be involved. All major organizations had members participating. It represented every facet of personality —the senses, the imagination, reason and intelligence, and feeling for what was happening. Existing in each major community project was a total outpouring of community spirit, focused, contained, and disciplined in a collective representation of the whole community.

Realization of Practical Accomplishments

Only after the excitement of demonstration had decreased, at least momentarily, could people realize fully what had happened and appreciate the work that had been done. There was some realization of the significance of what had been done in Eldorado when people saw that they had received the Freedom Foundation Award. But more important, perhaps, was the realization that came when people saw that certain of their fellow citizens who formerly had hated each other "with passion" were now seen to be sitting next to each other at a dinner quietly conversing and smiling. When Joe the plumber, and Jack the banker, could meet on the street and have something in common to talk about besides a leaky water faucet, this was sheer realization that it had worked, that it was real and not just a fantastic dream. The belief had now come to be possessed by those persons who had experienced the full run of the process and were now witnessing the fruits of it revealing itself throughout the community.

The Planning Process

There comes a time when these new ideas and new relationships must assume some stable form. They formalize into some steady pattern of life in the community, and they must become part of the larger social scene—we might even say, part of a still larger community. There must be some rational consideration of the ends and means of community development. Preparing for future activities in all phases of community life in light of the highest practical aims of local leaders is part of the planning process. It is a period of little public activity. The consultant concentrated on this phase following the formation of CDA, but the seeds were sown in the self-study period.

The fruits of the planning process came in the discipline of waiting for developments to unfold; there developed a quality of patience mixed with anticipation of events which would follow in the distant future. There were skills to accompany planning in every area of community life. There was a working knowledge of these areas which became part of the thinking of citizen planners. In Eldorado a specific group of men are armed with pertinent information for any inquiring industry, and many others have increased their understanding of the requirements of planning for economic development.

The way of doing and living "community" was coming to be felt strongly among those who had been in the center of activities from the beginning. The next step was the gradual diffusion of this condition throughout the remainder of the community. The consultant, along with leaders of the community, realized this would take years, perhaps a generation or more. The process by which this is accomplished is not yet fully known, but certain steps have been taken to make this possible.

Centering Down

To Eldorado leaders, this process of community development is more than a belief, it is a whole way of living *in* a community and a whole way of life *of* a community. The grasping of this concept takes time. It takes time first to "center down" into the life of individual people. It has already come a long way: We have noted how it was first encountered through the universally latent interest of people to improve themselves; how it then engaged people's imaginations and became tested subconsciously for consistency with the deeper traditions of the culture; how it then moved up through a new rationale and new symbols making the planning for action legitimate in the minds of leaders; and finally how it expressed itself through physical action and came to be realized through reflection on the fruits of that action. The process had an opportunity to be known in the thinking, feeling, and acting facets of the personalities of leading participants, and finally settled into a relatively permanent part of their everyday lives. But this is not to say that the process has centered down into the whole community, and that the whole community is prepared to perpetuate the things which were learned by the core participants and leaders. It is only to say that the diffusion of the process into all facets of the community is still going on in Eldorado.

By "centering down" is meant the way in which the process proceeds to become an established part of community life, so that it may be seen to continue over the years as an expression *of* the community. Eldorado has started on the road toward this end, but much of what is to be involved must remain speculative.

The process becomes established primarily through its own capacity to reproduce itself. That is, the patterns of the process must come to repeat themselves in such a way that new, untouched segments of the community become involved, and just as important, new generations of citizens may have an opportunity to participate in it. In the long run, the process may be seen as a cyclical affair, but one whose social form is broad and inclusive enough to meet the constantly evolving demands of a growing community.

In Eldorado several different associations were seen to develop to meet the demands of community survival. The major groups to form were the Chamber of Commerce, the Industrial Association, the Art Center, and the Community Development Association. Each one was set up to meet a fundamental need of community life as Eldorado people have defined it. Two major institutions which were created through the process were the summer Annual Picnic of CDA and the "town meeting." Today, program leaders say, "Whether or not the community development program will continue to renew itself is a matter for Eldorado people to demonstrate."

How can this process be analyzed?

EXPLANATIONS OF THE PROCESS

The actual process just described should be supported by theoretical constructs in the field of social work and sociology. The constructs ought to be adequate to explain and predict the behavior of the participants. Drawing from the facts of the story itself, the major stages and features of the process may be summarized as follows, using essentially the headings or areas under which the developments in Eldorado were discussed:

The Stages of Community Development

A. *A New Concept is Introduced*

1. Definition of the problem (challenge and response)
2. Tension and responsibility (new understanding)
3. Imaginative openings (change considered)
4. Development of confidence (change considered possible)
5. Release and renewal (change made acceptable)
6. Finding and facing the facts (technical knowledge acquired)

B. *The Possession of a Belief*

1. Total involvement in active demonstration
2. Realization of practical accomplishments
3. Community planning procedure initiated

C.   *The Centering Down of the Process*

1. Cyclical involvement of new persons in community development
2. Establishment of associations and institutions designed to carry the process into future generations

A Study in Meaning

The stages outlined above represent only one interpretation of what constitutes the "process" of community action.

The interpretation of process illustrates a problem in communication among the social scientist, the consultant, and the citizen. It conveys different meanings to each, depending upon his interests and relationship to community action. Different levels of explanation are illustrated in Diagram 1 and discussed in the following paragraphs.

The terms which were used to describe the action process in the earlier part of this study were "initiation, organization, execution, and maintenance." They were selected because they seemed most appropriate to express the model descriptions in the literature on community organization. This is the principal level of explanation for the professional consultant.

Action stages or phases may also be described in such abstract terms as "goal facilitation, legitimation, fulfillment of charter," etc.[4] This is the language of the social scientist and is indicative of his different perspective, for with this abstractness the perspective takes on an impersonal character and elements of the process appear determined by external forces rather than reflecting what happens when human beings enact the change themselves. To what extent the terms of the scientist become esoteric and completely separated from conventional usage depends upon the purposes of the analysis. It can make a great difference, then, whether the analyst is seeking to understand the internal changes of the community as a social system for its own sake with no practical applications in mind, or whether he may have some interest in communicating his knowledge to practitioners.

If the somewhat more practical interests of the consultant are involved, the analyst may shift to some extent into the lan-

Diagram 1.

COMMUNITY ACTION: LEVELS AND FOCUSES

THREE OBSERVERS: I. The Social Scientist   II. The Consultant   III. The Citizen

FOUR LEVELS: THE ANALYTICAL PROCESS   THE METHOD   THE PROGRAM   THE MOVEMENT

FIVE FOCUSES:

A. Community Focus	B. Consultant-Client Focus	C. Ideal Model Focus	D. Specific Focus	E. Personal Focus
1. Prior Situation	1. Development of Need for Change ("unfreezing")	1. Ideology	See Eldorado story for a description of a specific program	"Challenge"
2. Convergence of Interest (Initiating Set)	2. Establishment of Change Relationship	a. philosophy		"Response"
3. Goal Formulation (Charter)	3. Working Toward Change	b. objectives		"Tension"
4. Legitimacy and Support	a. Diagnosis of client system's problem	c. functions		"Understanding"
5. Goal Facilitation	b. Examination of alternative routes and goals	2. Mechanics		"Confidence"
6. Institutionalization	c. Establishing goals and intentions of action	a. initiation		"Responsibility"
	d. Transformation of intentions into actual change efforts	b. organization		"Renewal"
	4. Generalization and Stabilization of change	c. execution		
	5. Achieving a terminal relationship	d. maintenance		

guage of the consultant. An example of this may be found in the theory of Lippitt and associates who in one phase of their work concentrate upon the consultant-client relationship in analyzing stages of social change.[5] These stages (summarized in Diagram 1) are more readily understood conventionally yet still retain a definitely formal character which distinguishes the language of the scientist.

The stages of action just described in the Eldorado case study involved the personal experiences of key citizens and their consultant in the action program. The interpretation was made by the writer through talking with them about their program. The purpose was two-fold: first, to perceive and convey the feeling that made the experience real to them, and second, to provide the experience with some form and sequence. Some of the expressions were local ("confidence," "responsibility"), others were formed by the writer ("centering down," "release and renewal"), to convey more clearly what was perceived in the experience.

Leaders in this case were saying in effect: this is the *process* which people must go through if they want to remove strong emotional barriers to change. What it takes to break through such blockages as deep apathy and fear is confidence, imagination, tension, responsibility—these are the words that convey the meaning of their experience.

Although this description gives the process some form and sequence and provides a basis for generalization, it is not what would ordinarily be called "scientific" in the strict sense of the word. This account is perhaps more of a synthetic explanation of what happened than an analytical one. It is more of an idealistic description than what would be called a realistic one. Nevertheless it is one type of explanation that is important to understand in the field of community development.[6]

In another approach Irwin T. Sanders has suggested four ways of viewing community development: as a process, a method, a program, and a movement.[7] In the terms of our case study the community development *process* would best refer to the analytical stages of action, the *method* would refer to the ideal model followed by the consulting agency and the community,

the *program* would be the procedures outlined for taking action
in the particular community, and the *movement* would be the
dynamics as described locally in the Eldorado story where
people took hold of the "idea" of community development as the
basis for change.

Often the three observers (the scientist, consultant and citizen)
are so closely associated in field research that the concepts of one
perspective will diffuse into another. The terms employed
range from the highly abstract (the scientist) to the highly
personalized (the citizen), with the range in between undertaken
by the consultant according to his background and training. The
scientist is free to analyze the movement, the program, the
method, or the process, but has most often tended to center his
interest on the latter concept. This interest in process has already
diffused into the consultant orientation and is often communi-
cated to the citizen. The citizen can describe any aspects of
community action in his own terms if queried about it but
his normal interest is in the program and the interpersonal
relationships that develop in his own community. He is less
interested in generalizing (like the scientist) except in unusual
cases (such as Eldorado) where the interest may be picked up
from the orientation of the consultant. In this case generalization
did take place among the key leaders but retained a personal
emphasis.

Since there is such a close working relationship between these
three observers in the field of community development, the clear
definition of terms and the context in which they are used
become an important matter. Some concepts like "process,"
however, have come to be used currently by all three groups with
different meanings in each case. To add to the difficulties in
communication, the process concept is used differently by
observers within their own camp. The only solution to the
problem is to become aware of how different authors have used
the concept and to indicate which meaning is intended to each
context.

Murray G. Ross has used the term "process" to distinguish the
general orientation which the community takes in action. In his

text, Ross has distinguished five separate approaches to working with communities: 1) exploitive orientation, 2) reform orientation, 3) planning orientation, 4) process orientation, 5) therapy orientation. Ignoring the polar extremes (exploitive and therapy) he deals with the other three as positions which are frequently taken in approaching the community. Each has a different objective and methodology. The planning orientation begins with a "felt difficulty" and proceeds through a period of "exploration" to move toward a particular solution. The goal, however, is to secure a community plan in a problem area. The reform orientation begins with persons whose minds are made up with regard to a specific reform within the community and who then take steps through committee organization, sales and propaganda, to direct action. The process orientation is approached still differently:

> Here the purpose is to initiate a process. The process is one by which a community seeks to identify and take action with respect to its own problems. The purpose is not (as in the reform orientation) to take action to secure a specific reform, although this may at some point be involved; nor is it, as in the planning orientation, to plan in a particular problem area, although such planning may also be undertaken at some appropriate point. The purpose in the process orientation is to encourage the community itself to identify what it considers to be its problems and to work systematically on these problems; the underlying belief is that such an experience will increase the capacity of the community to deal with problems which will confront it in the future.[8]

In general, the "process" orientation outlined by Ross applies quite well to the approach made in the Eldorado case study. That is, the purpose of the approach was to increase the community's capacity to solve its own problems; the problem generalized by Ross as the "plight of mass man" was seen by the consultant as "a complete lack of community." The method consisted of "moving with the interests and needs of the community." The strategy, according to Ross, consisted of "encouraging community movement." These features were also part of the approach which was made in the Eldorado community.

A Study in Role Orientation

Although the orientation which the whole community assumed fits the expectations of community theorists, the role orientation of the consultant in the Eldorado story is not explained so easily. The particular form which it took contrasts sharply with the model which has been considered basic to describing the process in the field of social work. For instance, some of the principles which have been proposed to guide the community worker have been:

1. *The role of the professional worker should tend to be indirect in guiding a community program.*

> The professional worker is often spoken of as a leader. Is his position one of direct or indirect leadership? I think we will all recognize that statesmanship requires that he consciously assume an attitude of indirect leadership. . . . His assumption of direct leadership would attract to him other tasks and he would soon find himself loaded with responsibilities and surrounded by inactive associates.[9]

2. *The role of the professional consultant should be impersonal in his relations with the client and he should not identify himself with the community in any of its associations.*

> In the use of professional self, then, the social worker is acting in an impersonal relation to the client. The case worker is not serving in the role of "family friend" nor is the group worker a "big brother," or "big sister," to persons in the group. Similarly, the community organization worker must avoid a personal identification with groups or intergroups.[10]

3. *[Community organizers] seek to help people in terms of the values the people themselves hold and not in terms of the aims they set up "de novo."*[11]

4. *[The process of community organization] must deal with problems which the community recognizes as its problems.*[12]

5. *The consultant must work at a pace which is comfortable for the community.*[13]

Having made a detailed analysis of the consultant's orientation in the case study, we can say that the principles listed above are not without relevance in describing the role which he undertook.

At the same time we can say that these stated principles definitely do not characterize the emphasis which his role took in the community. As the consultant saw it, in order to change the "entrenched" social patterns which had developed in the community, he was forced to take *direct leadership* to initiate the process; he had to become *personal* with the community and its leaders and even to *identify* with the community's basic purposes; he had to express *new values*, create new ways for differing groups to associate with one another; and in the process of setting a pace for a community ("in need"), the consultant saw that some *discomfort* had to be experienced in making the transition to a new way of living and working together.

The principles guiding the consultant in the field of social work are not applicable to the case study of Eldorado. The study actually reveals an unorthodox approach to community organization.

A Study in Social Movement

The theoretical construct which appears most meaningful in sociological theory for examining the whole program is to be found in the field of social movements. The most fitting typology appears to be Herbert Blumer's original description of a "specific social movement."[14]

Blumer states that "social movements can be viewed as collective enterprises to establish a new order of life. They have their inception in a condition of unrest, and derive their motive power on the one hand, from wishes and hopes for a new scheme of living." Major features of what Blumer has described as characterizing a social movement are directly applicable to the Eldorado program. These features are outlined below:

1. *Stages of Development*
   a) Stage of social unrest
   b) Stage of popular excitement

  c) Stage of formalization
  d) Stage of institutionalization

2. *Mechanisms through which the movement grows and becomes organized*

  a) *Agitation*
    (1) Period which acts to loosen people's hold on previous attachments, awakens new impulses and ideas.
    (2) Leadership exists to intensify, release, and direct the tensions already present.

  b) *Esprit de Corps*
    (1) Its basis is constituted by a condition of rapport—feelings of intimacy and closeness sharing common experience—reinforcing the member's new conception of himself.
    (2) *Means of Development*
      (*a*) Informal Fellowship: singing, picnics, having fun, dancing.
      (*b*) Ceremonial Behavior: mass meetings, rallies, parades, huge demonstrations, and commemorative ceremonies which foster feelings of common identity and sympathy, slogans, songs, etc.

  c) *Development of Morale*
    (1) While *esprit de corps* gives enthusiasm, vigor and life to the movement, *morale* gives persistency and determination; its test is adversity, met by group will.
    (2) Faith or conviction in the ultimate attainment, by the movement, of its goal.

  d) *Development of an ideology*
    (1) Ideology consists of a body of doctrine and beliefs.
    (2) Ideology has a two-fold character:
      (*a*) Much of it is erudite and scholarly, in response to outside intellectuals, as a defensible position in the world of higher learning.
      (*b*) Other forms are "popular" in the form of folk

arguments which present the tenets of the movement for ready comprehension and comsumption
by the public.

Although these features are listed as being reproduced in the
Eldorado program, there were certain characteristics omitted
from this brief summary because they did not seem to fit the
evidence which was available in the case study. These points are
listed below.[15]

In-Group and Out-Group

Blumer points out that the necessity of two groups coming to
identify each other as enemies is part of the developing *esprit de
corps*. "The out-group is regarded as unscrupulous and vicious,
and is felt to be attacking the values which the in-group holds
dear."[16]

In creating the orientation for the program, the consultant had
defined the enemies of the community as "apathy and indifference." This was "attacked," and leaders were sometimes fustrated
by those who "could not be moved." The narrative indicates the
consultant's own frustration with those who were not touched by
the program. However, this was not part of the value orientation
and accepted as such. As has been noted, there was never any
open segmented opposition to the program. The writer did not
find that the belief in an enemy (in the form of persons or
groups) was a distinctive feature of either the process orientation
or the morale of program leaders.

Sacred Objects

Part of the development of "morale," as Blumer defines it, is the
emergence of a "saint cult" with a major saint and several minor
saints who become deified and endowed with miraculous powers.
Blumer also mentions the emergence of a sacred literature.

It has already been pointed out that there were individuals
who constructed a special image of the consultant out of their
own needs, but to the writer's knowledge this consisted of only
one or two individuals, not the present leadership. Leaders expressed considerable respect for the consultant, but not in the

sense that Blumer describes as typical of the movement. The consultant's own books and writings were considered highly important during the initial phases of the program. If other material of a contradictory sort had been submitted by someone other than the consultant during this period, they probably would have been rejected. However, this was considered essential to setting the process in motion. There was no evidence to indicate that these materials were considered by groups as "sacred literature," as Blumer has described them.[17]

Well-Defined Goal

A specific movement is viewed by Blumer as having a well-defined goal. An example would be the antislavery movement as it sought to emancipate the slaves, or woman's suffrage as the privilege of voting was sought. The value orientation which was described in the case study indicates that the goal was diffuse. Emphasis was placed upon concrete values which were considered universally important to people living in democratic communities, but the consultant laid no claim upon knowing the ideal state of the community insofar as its institutional or organizational form was concerned. The forms were left to evolve out of the process itself as local people in a unique community were to come together to make them possible.[18]

Reform or Revolutionary Type

Types of specific social movements which Blumer describes are "reform" and "revolutionary." Neither type is described in such a way that the features are applicable to the distinctive features of the Eldorado program. For example, it was *not* like a revolutionary movement in the sense that it sought to divide the community into the "haves" and the "have-nots," or that it was likely to be "driven underground," or that it sought to agitate the depressed and "make converts rather than develop a public opinion in favor of its program." It was like the reform movement which Blumer describes, in the sense that it accepted the basic tenets and mores of the existing order, and used them against the social defects which they were attacking. However, it was *not* like the reform movement in that it did not seek to change only some "specific phase or limited area of the social order" of the community.[19]

Perhaps a principal reason for the difficulty in finding a fully adequate typology is that the theory of social movements has developed from evidence acquired from movements occurring on the level of society, rather than on the level of community.[20] Movements on a community level may prove to rule out many of the necessary features which have appeared to be part of social movements on the societal level.

For example, all movements described in the literature have competing or opposing movements with which to contend. Resistance arose in each one of our case studies, but in no case was there open organized resistance, nor were there other organized groups competing for "converts," as is the case of many movements which span a society, such as communism, fascism, or other "isms" which have existed in many religious movements. Each of these movements faces an outer enemy and tends to develop a strong system of defenses, much as Blumer describes them. However, the Eldorado program (and others of its kind) are developing with the actual cooperation of external systems, rather than in the face of their competition. These programs so design themselves within the internal system of the community that they do not acquire strong competitive features in relation to other associations in the community. Their greatest danger does not lie in being overcome by a greater organized power so much as it lies in the sheer apathy and disinterest which come to attend them in later years.[21]

We may conclude that Blumer's typology of social movements helped to explain some of the stages and mechanisms of growth which were evident in the Eldorado case study. However, there were significant features missing which made the typology inapplicable.

The sequence of events which took place in the Eldorado case study serves as a unique model of rapid social change guided by an outside educational agency. The process contains significance both for the theory of social change and for professional work in the field of community organization and development.

Notes

1. The use of the word "community" in this section reflects its use among local citizens. That is, it expresses the opinion of the persons involved (core leaders) as to what most of the people in the town think or feel. The purpose in this section is not to determine the validity of these statements; it is only to reflect the meaning of the program as the consultant and local leaders have conceived it.

2. In several instances, local citizens specified dramatic changes in personality resulting from participation in the program.

3. Historic accounts of the nature of charismatic leadership seem to support this point. The leader is understood to be "fulfilling the scriptures," rather than breaking them. This interpretation of change, if universally applicable, would assume that lodged within the traditions of any culture, there lie those sacred elements which serve as the basis for transforming the structure of the community.

4. Paul A. Miller, *Community Health Action: A Study of Community Contrast* (Michigan State University Press, 1953), pp. 13-18; Christopher Sower, John Holland, Kenneth Tiedke, and Walter Freeman, *Community Involvement: The Web of Formal and Informal Ties* (Glencoe, Illinois: The Free Press, 1957), pp. 308-14; Charles R. Hoffer, "Social Action in Community Development," *Rural Sociology*, Volume 23, No. 1 (March, 1958), p. 43; Harold F. Kaufman, "Toward an Interactional Conception of Community," *Social Forces*, Vol. 38, No. 1 (October, 1959), p. 13; George Beal and Harold Capener, "A Social Action Model," a paper presented at the Rural Sociological Society Meeting, Pullman, Washington, August, 1958; John S. Holik, "Small Community Development Process: An Action Model," a paper presented at the program of the Committee on Community Research and Development of the Society for the Study of Social Problems, August 28, 1961, Chase Park Plaza Hotel, St. Louis, Missouri; James Green and Selz C. Mayo, "A Framework for Research in the Actions of Community Groups," *Social Forces*, Vol. 31, No. 4 (May, 1953), pp. 323-26; Frank H. Sehnert, "The Community Development Process Within a Procedural Framework," *Adult Leadership Magazine*, Vol. 8, No. 9 (March, 1960), pp. 262-64.

5. Ronald Lippitt, *et al., The Dynamics of Planned Change* (New York: Harcourt, Brace and Company, 1958), pp. 130-43.

6. The personal character of this account suggests the fields of psychology or social psychology as likely fields of analysis. To follow the behavioral traditions of these sciences would require moving to another level of explanation which would convey a different meaning. Within different psychological schools of thought there exist such analytical constructs as: stimulus-response, catharsis, transference,

frustration-aggression, etc. Unfortunately the danger in moving from one level of explanation to another is that some concepts may appear applicable when they are not. The validity of a psychological analysis may suffer from the fact that the concepts are drawn from the study of animal behavior or from a school of thought deriving its frame of reference from abnormal behavior.

7. Irwin T. Sanders, *Community* (The Ronald Press Co., 1958), pp. 406-7.

8. Murray Ross, *Case Histories in Community Organization* (New York: Harper & Brothers, 1958). See following pages for further description of methodology.

9. George L. Warren, (an article in *The Family*, November, 1930) quoted in Clarence King, *Organizing for Community Action* (New York: Harper & Brothers, 1948), pp. 11-12.

10. Campbell Murphy, *Community Organization Practice* (Boston: Houghton Mifflin Co., 1954), p. 93.

11. Herbert Stroup, *Social Work* (American Book Company, 1948), p. 20.

12. Murray Ross, *op. cit.*, p. 13.

13. *Ibid.*

14. Herbert Blumer, "Social Movements," in *New Outlines of the Principles of Sociology*, ed. Alfred Lee (New York: Barnes & Noble Inc., 1946). The descriptive outline which follows is taken from this chapter, pp. 199-221.

15. Some of the interpretations made in this section are based upon interview data not included in the narrative or description of the "Process orientation."

16. Blumer, *op. cit.*, p. 206

17. These conclusions are qualified in two respects: 1) the period of study may be considered a relatively short time with regard to what may be required for a social movement to evolve, and 2) "sacred" is a concept relative to a continuum of emotional intensity upon which other points must be identified in comparison or contrast to it. It is only in this way that the concept may take on meaning. The examples which were offered by Blumer (*Mein Kampf, Das Capital*, writings of Mary Baker Eddy, etc.) do not have the same reference in this case. The terms which the writer has sought to use are those which he heard expressed in interviews and appears to describe more adequately the relationship established.

18. Although a number of the associational forms which were created in this case study (CDA, the Industrial Association, the Art Center, etc.) were brought into being with the assistance of the consultant, the process orientation emphasizes the importance of these forms being created out of the needs of a particular locality as people come to define them. The fact that other communities in which

the "process" has been applied (e. g., Cobden) have developed different forms is more conclusive evidence that the goal in "form" is diffuse.

19. In a recent text on collective movements, a typological description is offered that is suggestive of the action taken in the case study. The Eldorado program would be understood as "Respectable-nonfactional" whose type of opposition consisted of "disinterest and token support" and whose means of operation was "legitimate." However, the description is not developed beyond these points and no further application can be made. Ralph Turner and Lewis Killian, *Collective Behavior* (Englewood Cliffs, N. J.: Prentice-Hall, 1957), p. 329.

20. Professor Ernest Shideler has sought to distinguish these levels of social movement by the terms "micro" and "macro" social movements. More study is required at the micro movement level to describe adequately the stages of action. For one study of micro movements see: William R. Arnold, *Social Movements of Parents in Five Communities For Better Care of Mentally Retarded Children*, M. A. thesis, University of Illinois, 1956.

21. We also might hypothesize that the greater the number of people involved, the greater the need for sacred collective symbols and sacred literature to retain the intensity of loyalty required. The more people involved, the greater the distances, and the more difficult it becomes to maintain the sentiment (so accessible in person-to-person relations in a small community) which binds people together and gives the movement its motivating force.

APPENDIX

THE COMMUNITY MOVEMENT IN THE UNITED STATES

AN HISTORICAL NOTE

The growth of community councils, community centers and welfare agencies, community planning commissions, university-community programs, etc., are all recent manifestations of a long-range interest in the local settlement, rather than the state, the region, or the nation, as the locus for studying and treating human problems and working toward a better way of life. There has been a long history of such interests in America, dating back to the early communitarian settlements and extending forward to the present complex assortment of community-oriented programs.

This history has the characteristics of a "general social movement." It has no definite organization of its own. It has no specific leaders guiding it as a whole. It has moved in a slow, halting manner, yet for over a century there has been a continuous, visible surging upward, in multifarious ways, of a vital interest in the local settlement as the context for meaningful social action and study.

The community movement has witnessed many specific social movements. Early in this history, these movements seemed to have origins independent of each other arising from dissatisfactions with the society-at-large. Later, however, these movements evidenced more interdependence as new submovements grew out of the merging of their several interests.

Currently there are signs of a developing interest in bringing together the many separate modern approaches to community action and integrating them in a new specific movement. This trend of thought is coming to be called "community development."

In view of the current interests in communities and community action, it seems appropriate to review briefly some of the key periods which together constitute the history behind modern approaches to community action. Different periods of this history are well covered in separate sources but it seems important to condense and review this knowledge in order to see the over-all picture of the search for community in the American setting.[1]

Communitarian Settlements

The earliest manifestation of the thinking in the reformist phase of the community movement is traceable to the well-known communitarian movement in the early part of the nineteeth century.[2] Taking their ideals from the Protestant Reformation and the Utopian socialist theory, many cooperative settlements were founded in America on a truly community-centered basis. Some of the Utopian thought which gave rise to these settlements contained such principles as these:

1. Society should not be conceived of as comprising only a group of separate individuals, but rather as groups of associations related to one another. The association (such as the community) is the fundamental unit of society.

2. A fever of centralization is sweeping the world. What is needed is decentralization of power into smaller communal units, where true authority and responsibility for living can be exercised.

3. Only the free, voluntary association of people can solve the great organic problem of society; social change must take place gradually, starting at the local levels and moving toward the top levels of society.

These were a few of the principles found in such writers as Proudhon, Fourier, Owen, Kropotkin, Babeuf, and Landauer.[3] Owen had the means and the determination to see his beliefs put into action in the United States where he formed a series of cooperative settlements.

Other leaders, religiously and intellectually motivated, did the same. The community experiments derived from the intellectual tradition did not last long. The religiously motivated experiments fared better; some of them still exist today. Henrik Infield describes the number of experiments involved in this movement in the following excellent summary.

In the United States, 262 cooperative communities are known to have been established—some of them merely branches of larger settlements. Similar groups, though fewer in number, have been organized in Europe. Both in America and elsewhere, for the most part, these experiments have been short-lived. According to statistics compiled by Lee Emerson Deets, on 130 settlements, 91 lasted less than a decade, 59 less than five years, 50 only two years, and 32 only one year. The life of some of the more intellectual experiments, like New Harmony, Indiana, Brook Farm, Massachusetts, and the Oneida Colony, New York State, was so brief that they belong definitely to the 19th century past.

A small percentage of these groups, however, have persisted more than a century. Of these, three have been disbanded: Ephrata Cloister, Pennsylvania, which existed 173 years (1732-1905); the Shaker Communities, settled in various states of the U.S.A. (1778-ca. 1940); and the Harmonists, or Rappists, whose settlements, in Pennsylvania and Indiana, lasted a hundred years (1805-1905). Three other communities, with records that go back to the 18th century (one of them to the 16th century), have continued to the present day; the Amana Community, Iowa, founded in Europe in 1714, and moved to the United States in 1842; the Doukhobors, organized in Russia about the middle of the 18th century, who settled in Canada (ca. 1879), where they still live in several cooperative communities; and, finally, the Hutterites, whose significant group originated in Moravia in 1528. The Hutterites came to the United States in 1874. They live in fifty communites in South Dakota, Montana, and Canada (Manitoba and Alberta).[4]

The interest in creating cooperative settlements in this Utopian tradition has never died out. Such planned communities are still being created. A loose federation of such groups is still in existence and is called the Fellowship of Intentional Communities.[5]

The Garden City movement, a variant of the cooperative or communitarian movement of the last century, arose from the literary social criticism of such men as John Ruskin, Thomas Carlyle, and Charles Dickens. At the turn of the century, Ebenezer Howard, moved by the depressing conditions of the cities, wrote a book called *Tomorrow*, which set forth the idea of the Garden City. In this Utopian description the residences were to be distributed about a large central court in which public buildings would be located. The shopping center would be on the edge of town and industries on the outskirts. Land would remain in single ownership of the community. This movement had some influence on city planning in the United States, but the major effect remained in England where several communities were modeled directly from Howard's design.[6] The movement in America entered another phase in response to the demands of new social and demographic conditions.

The New Social Setting

The early American communities were in many ways very different from one another. Besides unique Utopian settlements there were the more common New England towns with their central squares, their town meetings, their churches, schools, their occupational divisions—politicians, lawyers, blacksmiths, carriage-makers, etc. There were also plantation systems (each one virtually self-sufficient) with their patriarchal systems, structuring and providing for the intimate way of life that arises in relative isolation. There were small county seat towns, which struggled for survival in the semi-wilderness of the Midwest.

The features held in common among these diverse settlements were not apparent until the appearance of large cities. With urbanization came a loss of control over community life, a loss of a sense of togetherness and intimacy of living grounded in an area with which people could commonly identify. It was in this changing context that the next phase of the community movement began to take form. While this history is well known, it is necessary to review those sociological conditions which seem pertinent to explaining the search for community.

In the decades following the Civil War, the whole institutional and demographic character of the United States was undergoing revolutionary changes. Great advances were being made in technology and industry. Communication and transportation lines were advancing everywhere; new factories and industrial plants were rapidly being located in cities across the country. Corporate business was expanded to great proportions under the thrust of the new ideology—free enterprise. The country was open to anyone who had the incentive to make a million dollars. Immigrants flowed into urban areas, and cities stretched forth, moving like slumbering giants to dominate the regions about them.

Out of this social-economic-political context came social problems of great magnitude. Industrial corporations, gaining tremendous monarchal power, produced, along with material comforts, vast inequalities between poverty and wealth. The new technology swept away the laborer's sense of responsibility and pride in craftsmanship, so basic to his identity in the social-economic organization of earlier periods. Gigantic bureaucracies rose to add to the growing complexities of the economy; the requirements of large, formal hierarchical systems broke up the close personal relationships of workers and substituted impersonal rules and regulations as the basis of working together. Technical communication advanced, but cultural communication broke down. People became mobile at an unheard-of rate. The local school systems and municipal governments were slow to respond to the changing scene; they could barely count the new settlements of people and keep up with the adjustments of the moment, much less plan the future of the community.

Two prominent social problems arose in this period. Both emerged from conditions outside the local community, but their solutions came to be defined in the context of the community. One problem was *poverty* and its associated problems which resulted from the inequalities the economy had produced in the distribution of wealth; the other was *culture conflict* which resulted from high rates of immigration and internal migration.

It was largely in an effort to eliminate the problem of poverty that the charity movement began in American communities. The settlement movement was started largely out of an attempt to eliminate culture conflict. In the latter part of the nineteenth century both movements poured workers into communities to treat these and associated problems. Together they created the conditions for the rise of the community organization movement.

The Charity and Settlement Movements

The cause of poverty was not interpreted as an outgrowth of the economic order. The source of the problem, it was said, was a defect in the character of the individual ("pauperism") and the means of correcting it was by way of philanthropy, friendly counsel, and the coordination of community agencies for the charitable dispensing of money.

The community welfare council is a uniquely American creation. It emerged from professional efforts of charity workers to deal with a complex pattern of social organization involving hundreds of public and private voluntary agencies serving the community. The charity organization movement laid the groundwork for this method of community action.

Like the charity movement, the settlement movement originated in England. The first London settlement was called Toynbee Hall. The first settlement in the United States is generally recognized to be the Neighborhood Guild, established in New York City in 1877. A few years later Hull House was founded in Chicago by Jane Addams and Ellen Gates Starr. The settlement movement quickly spread to other cities.

The beliefs supporting the early movement rested on the following premises:

1. Underprivileged people need to be reached directly and personally in the community or neighborhood in which they live. Locally housed and supported organizations can better deal with the problems in the context from which they arise.

2. A major problem of our cities stems from the influx of immigrants who are unaccustomed to the American way of life. They need financial help, but still more they need fellowship, recreation, and education in the civic responsibilities and cultural opportunities of America.

3. The settlement is the means of bridging the gap between the

social classes, of bringing the wealthy and the poor together, and thus "socializing democracy."

4. Wherever possible, it is important to institute social reform with respect to housing, unsanitary conditions, low wages, and other undesirable conditions.

The importance of the settlement movement in paving the road to more modern approaches to the community cannot be underestimated. Jesse Steiner has this to say:[7]

> The social settlement has been the agency through which the community movement first expressed itself. The first community workers were enrolled largely from residents in the settlement. Those interested in play grounds, night classes, vocational education, library extension, work for immigrants, etc., found the settlement in the improvement of social conditions unquestioned. Without doubt the modern emphasis upon community organization can quite largely be regarded as a logical outgrowth of the efforts of the settlements to direct attention to the value of the neighborhood as a social unit.

The charity and settlement movements had many similarities; often the objects of their interest would closely parallel one another. At the same time each had a certain distinctiveness which each sought to maintain, and the cross-criticisms among workers in each movement were early forecasts of problems which professional community action approaches are still confronting. Settlement workers considered charity people as the "outsiders," bending down to help people of lower quality than themselves. They said one must live with the poor before one can come to know them and eventually aid them; "slumming," allegedly a practice of the very rich, was looked upon disdainfully by neighborhood social workers. On the other hand, charity people would assert that settlement people were "intruders," not really an accepted part of the community. They said that attempts to "Americanize" the immigrant did him an injustice and brought on only further resistance and rebellion which complicated the problem. However, both movements withstood the strain of criticism remarkably well, and served as a stimulus to many other social movements appearing at the turn of the century.

Other Movements

Many new movements arose simultaneously at the turn of the century, seeking local chapters to further their national programs. Some of these localized movements, in both their general and specific form, were: the mental health movement, the voluntary organization movement, the labor movement, the youth movement (including the child labor movement and the establishment of local youth agencies such as the YMCA and the Boy Scouts), the recreation movement, the country-life movement, women's suffrage movement, the cooperative movement, the welfare movement (including the public services movement, family welfare, child welfare, etc.), and others.

The professional focus on the community began to sharpen and served as a focal point around which many more specific community movements began to form: the community center movement, the school-community movement, the community-chest movement, the community council movement, the community survey movement, and the community organization movement. The "community" came to stimulate both the scientific and the humanistic interests of professional people and soon became a basic part of higher education.

ACADEMIC APPROACH TO THE COMMUNITY

Academic interest in the nature of the community began with the nineteeth-century initiators of sociological typologies which described the historical transition of one form of collective life to another: status-contract (Henry Maine); *gemeinschaft-gesellschaft* (Ferdinand Tönnies); mechanical-organic (Emile Durkheim) and others. The turn of the century, however, witnessed a trend away from the historical and philosophical emphasis of the grand theorists toward empirical research in specific communities. This trend, which has continued to the present time, has gone through several phases.

The community studies conducted at the beginning of the

century contained the ruralist philosophy and reform spirit of the previous century; however, soon after World War II, studies took on a more analytical orientation. Robert E. Park was a major figure linking the grand theory of the previous century with the new analytical movement to study the community in terms of its ecological structure.[8]

> The community, if not always identical with society, is, at the very least, the habitat in which alone societies grow up. It provides the economic organization and the necessary conditions in which societies are rooted; upon which, as upon a physical base, they can be established.
>
> This is one reason why sociological research may very properly begin with the community. A more practical reason is the fact that the community is a visible object. One can point it out, define its territorial limits, and plot its constituent elements, its population, and its institutions on maps. Its characteristics are more susceptible to statistical treatment than society, in the sense of Comte.

Several trends followed. The next distinctive period began in the 1930's with the publication of *Middletown*, which stressed (in addition to the ecological orientation) a structural and typological approach to the community.[9] A dominating interest of community research in succeeding decades was in the study of the class structure. Typical of this emphasis was Lloyd Warner's "Yankee City" series. Finally in the last decade (1950's) several studies have indicated a new trend in the making— that of studying the process of community action. Hunter, Miller, Sowers, *et al.*, have each conducted studies of local health councils in action.

The concept of community has proven to have a wealth of meaning. It is one of those great words, like "love" or "truth," whose definition is inexhaustible and significant for every period of man's history. It is continuing to reveal its special meaning to those in almost every field of the social sciences and humanities. Social philosophers such as Brownell, Buber, Morgan and Nisbet, have explored its importance both as an existential fact and as the foundation of a healthy society. Social scientists have picked up other themes. Hobhouse saw in community an evolutionary principle, Hiller saw community as a form of social group,

Arensberg saw in it a method of analysis, Redfield saw it as the major focus of anthropological research.

An abbreviated listing of some of the academic studies of the community (in chronological order) follows below. While the early studies were directed toward rural community life it is noteworthy that a significant number of texts appeared later under the title of community which dealt with life in the metropolis. The selection includes some texts which have a philosophical or social work emphasis, but the main body of works are descriptive accounts of localities with a view to understanding them as communities.

Community Studies[10]

1904	*The Sociology of a New York City Block*—Jones
1906	*An American Town*—Williams
1907	*Quaker Hill*—Wilson
1909	*The Study of the Population of Manhattanville*—Wooston
1912	*A Hoosier Village*—Sims
....	*The Evolution of the Country Community*—Wilson
1915	*The Rural Community*—Galpin
1916	*Essentials of Community Efficiency*—Shephard
1920	*Community Organization*—Hart
1920	*Locating the Country Community*—Sanderson
....	*The Rural Community*—Sims
....	*Community*—McIver
1921	*The Community*—Lindeman
....	*Rural Community Organization*—Hayes
1922	*The Farmer and His Community*—Sanderson
1925	*Community Organization*—Steiner
....	*Surveying Your Community*—Brunner
1926	*The Urban Community*—Burgess
1927	*Village Communities*—Brunner
1928	*The American Community in Action*—Steiner
....	*Community Problems*—Wood
....	*Case Studies in Community Organization*—Petit
....	*The Ghetto*—Wirth
1929	*The Gold Coast and the Slum*—Zorbaugh
....	*Middletown*—Lynd

1931 *The Community and Social Welfare*—North
1932 *The Rural Community*—Sanderson
.... *Family and Community Life in Ireland*—
Arensberg-Kimball
1933 *The Metropolitan Community*—McKenzie
.... *Community and Society*—Osborn and Neumeyer
1935 *Deep South*—Davis and Gardners
.... *Series of Community Profiles*—Taylor
1937 *Middletown in Transition*—Lynds
.... *Caste and Class in Southern Town*—Dollard
.... *St. Denis*—Miner
1938 *The Changing Community*—Zimmerman
.... *Community Backgrounds of Education*—Cook
1939 *Rural Community Organization*—Sanderson and Polson
.... *Your Community*—Colcord
1940 *Tenants of the Almighty*—Raper
1941 *Elmtown's Youth*—Hollingshead
.... *Plainville*—West
.... *The Social Life of a Modern Community*—Warner
1942 *The Small Community*—Morgan
1943 *Toward Community Understanding*—Blackwell
1944 *Life in a Mexican Village*—Lewis
1945 *Democracy in Jonesville*—Warner
1946 *Small Communities in Action*—Ogdens
1947 *The Community*—Kinneman
1948 *Community Recreation*—Meyer and Brightbill
.... *The Structure of the Metropolitan Community*—Bogue
1949 *American Community Behavior*—Bernard
1950 *The Human Community*—Brownell
.... *Community Organization and Planning*—Hillman
.... *Small Town Renaissance*—Poston
1951 *Social History of a War Boom Community*—
Havighurst and Morgan
1952 *Human Communities*—Park
.... *Community Power Structure*—Hunter
1953 *Approaches to Community Development*—Ruopp
.... *Community Health Action*—Miller
1954 *Community Organization and Practice*—Murphy

1955   *The Little Community*—Redfield
....   *Community Conflict*—Coleman
1956   *Community Organization: Action and Inaction*—Hunter
....   *The American Community*—Mercer
....   *Crestwood Heights*—Seeley, Sims, Loosely
1957   *Community Involvement*—
            Sower, Holland, Tiedke, Freeman
1958   *Small Town in Mass Society*—Vidich and Bensman
....   *The Community*—Sanders
....   *Case Histories in Community Organization*—Ross
1959   *Community Structure and Analysis*—Sussman
1960   *Community Structure and Change*—
            Nelson, Ramsey, Vernor
....   *The Eclipse of Community*—Stein
1961   *Community Political Systems*—Janowitz

The separation which has existed between the study of the community and the practice of community organization may be partly due to the social scientist's holding fast to "unalterably" fixed scientific procedures and to what he considered "objectivity," in opposition to the practitioner's personal involvement and attachment to "unalterable" fixed social practices, sometimes dictated by the requirements of state governments. It may also be due to the conventional separation that has always tended to exist between town and gown. Nevertheless, the parallel lines of interest in the community are reaching an infinitive point, so to speak, where they are drawing nearer to each other.

The College and the Community

Following World War II there appeared in different educational settings across the country efforts to bridge this separation. The efforts were not nationally organized, there was no central information agency to communicate what was happening; yet, evidence mounted that higher education was beginning to develop new programs relating the campus to community life. The departments within specific colleges and universities which initiated this type of approach varied considerably from one institution to the next. On the university level, extension services could be found reporting new programs in consultation with communities of the state;[11] sometimes academic departments within a college would initiate the relationship; sometimes whole colleges reported changes in their curriculum and administration to account for a new educational philosophy which included the training of students on the community level.[12] These sources began sending forth newsletters and reports of their progress in this new venture; some universities and colleges held joint conferences on college-community problems.

Several years ago this writer collected many of the annual reports made by these institutions and recorded their statements of purpose. The following statement summarizes some of the ideas contained in the efforts of those making their approach to the community in the context of liberal education.[13]

> There are three general characteristics of these approaches which are beginning to draw them together and set them apart in type from other educational approaches. First is the conviction that training in human relations is basic to the educational process. Part of this conviction is the awareness that every student will be confronting problems of human relationships no matter what occupation or position in society he assumes. A second characteristic exists in the growing recognition that each college and university has a responsibility to its community and its region. It must actively respond to the needs of its area and participate in cooperative efforts to improve community life. A third characteristic that has evolved is the recognition that the community or region may serve as the ground for a more realistic education for students in the varied disciplines. In the community, the student must deal with a reality which the campus itself cannot provide. Field work adds to his total educational experience; it can challenge him to another level of learning.

The educational institutions engaged in these approaches to the community have drawn upon the field of community organization. This field has had a development of its own which it behooves us to trace in bringing to a conclusion this review of movements taking place at the community level.

COMMUNITY ORGANIZATION

Community organization emerged from the convergence of two other movements that appeared between 1900 and World War I. One is the community survey movement, and the other, the community council movement. It is necessary to treat each separately to understand the product of the two movements. Since the community council plays such an important role in the comparative study of this text, considerable attention will be given to its historical development.

The Community Survey Movement

Not long after the turn of the century, in 1907, the economy of the country was jolted, rising abruptly and then falling and producing considerable unemployment. Not only were charity and settlement agencies reactivated by the problems created from the economic strain, but a new practical approach to community betterment was initiated. People were coming to believe that the local community had a responsibility to deal with these problems by studying itself scientifically.

The establishment of the Russell Sage Foundation proved to be the beginning of the community survey movement. One of the first acts of the new foundation was to grant a subsidy toward financing a survey of Pittsburgh. This was begun in 1907 as a socio-economic analysis of an industrial district in that city. It served as a classic model for many surveys taken subsequently in other cities.

The community survey movement did not arise purely out of academic interest. As Jesse Steiner reports, its promoters were practical men of affairs, genuinely interested in community improvement. The consequences of this fact are noteworthy.[14]

Consequently the survey was never regarded as successful unless public opinion was aroused to the point where community action was made possible along lines recommended in the survey report. Its leaders always insisted that the work of the survey had not been completed until its recommendations had been

shaped into a community program and arrangements made for
putting this program into effect. Since this was the impelling
motive behind the survey movement, it was inevitable that it
should become an important factor in the field of community
organization. As a matter of fact, long before its real significance
in this connection was fully realized, it was building up a
technique of approach to communities without which the
modern community organization movement would have been impossible.

The survey links the community organization movement
historically to the academic approach and to the city planning
movement. However, in the first half of the twentieth century the
community council became the "method" of community organization, and the survey only one of several techniques to be
initiated by the council.

Community Council Movement

In the early decades of the twentieth century there was great
proliferation of social agencies of all kinds purporting to serve
the community. At that time social work was emerging as a
professional field and equipping itself to meet the needs of the
times. It moved into already established areas such as children's
courts, hospital social services, and psychiatric clinics, increasing the personnel of these agencies and adding new services
and agencies of their own. These new services compounded the
difficulties of communication already existing in the complex
conditions of social services.

One of the first efforts to coordinate the many unrelated
private and public services centered on raising money for the
separate agencies. Thus the Community Chest movement can be
seen as another forerunner of the community council. Denver
was the first city to initiate such a program when, in 1888, a
number of service agencies united their appeals for funds and
called the combination the Charity Organization Society.

The power and influence of the national charity organization
was at that time very strong; this strength continued through the
turn of the century, and most efforts to coordinate services were

reported as taken under the auspices of charity societies. Gradually, as the positions of other professional organizations in the community became stronger, the position of the charity organization society was challenged. A crucial period of struggle for control over setting standards in social welfare appeared in different communities. Bruno describes how this critical point was passed at the professional level and how an important change in policy took place to help solve the growing problem.[15]

> Credit for finding a solution should probably be given to Francis H. McLean, associate director of the charity organization department of the Russell Sage Foundation, for his suggestion that the two functions be separated: the charity organization should concentrate on its services to families; and to set standards, there should be a new organization, to be called a "central council of social agencies," composed of representatives of social agencies that wished to unite in a common project of establishing and improving standards, thereby taking the ungracious and impractical responsibility of setting standards away from a single agency, and placing it upon the entire group. This was, obviously, the only pragmatic method of doing the job, but its suggestion was evidence of the democratic faith of McLean in the integrity of the individual agencies.

The first councils of social agencies which were organized for the purpose of coordinating the activities of the social agencies were in Pittsburgh and Milwaukee.[16] Both appeared in 1909. Following this beginning, the movement of councils across the United States is difficult to sketch because of the lack of historical records. Most surveys have favored counting the number of councils organized in urban areas, but the movement has developed an untold number of councils in small communities.[17]

Following the Pittsburgh–Milwaukee beginning, the appearance of councils increased in number throughout communities across the nation. In 1917 seven cities had established city-wide councils. Then with entry into World War I, the number suddenly rose dramatically when the need for coordinated community services was defined as critical to national defense. The speed and efficiency with which councils were organized and put into effect at this time was perhaps indicative of their natural capacity to deal with critical situations. Basing his information on circulars issued by the Council of National Defense between May, 1918 and January, 1919, Kenneth Beam reports:[18]

> A circular dated May 11, 1918 reports forty-one State Councils as acting favorably on the plan for organizing Community Councils. Of the seven other states five reported they had already developed systems of defense councils so similar as to make new organizations inadvisable. . . . A Circular dated October 1, 1918, reported 20 states with 100% community council organization. . . .

According to Johns and DeMarche, by 1923 councils "were functioning in twenty of the larger cities and in many smaller communities."[19] From this point on to the mid-1930's, there is no clear picture to be drawn on the number of councils organized. Before 1935, survey findings reported councils organized in ninety-five cities and towns, in twelve states. Over three hundred councils were reported in 1937; in 1938, between 350 and 380 coordinating councils were reported in twenty-nine states.[20]

In the summer of 1939 a comprehensive survey was made by the American Legion national headquarters. They sought an answer to the question: "Are there any coordinated councils or similar activities functioning in your state or the communities of your state?" The replies indicated that there were 598 councils in twenty-four states. The report noted that such a survey does not reach many rural communities and neighborhood councils in larger cities and if the count had been extended to them, the number would have easily run over a thousand, taking into consideration every state in the union.[21]

Special surveys have been conducted in Michigan under the supervision of Howard McClusky in an effort to determine the nature of the council movement. He had this to say:[22]

> In recent years the community council movement in Michigan has had an interesting development. It is estimated that approximately 120 councils have existed at some time during the 1936-46 decade. According to our data, the greatest number operating in any one year during this period was 55 in 1954. Evidently 1939, 1940, and 1943 were years of active organization. The decline in the formation of new councils after 1943

has since been followed by a lively resumption of organization in 1947 and 1948. Sixty-six councils are known by the writer to be in various stages of existence in April, 1949.

As implied by the preceding data, community councils come and go. It is estimated that 59% of the 120 councils in existence between 1939 and 1946 at some time ceased operation. The average life of this vanishing 59% was two years, one-third of which lasted less than a year. On the other hand, an important number of councils continued during the same period without interruption, and others have returned to vigorous life after a period of suspended activity. As in the case of many enterprises dependent on voluntary services, the mortality rate of community councils is high, as is the revival rate.

By the time of World War II, the number of agency services in communities had increased still further in number, and cities had continued to develop councils on a neighborhood basis. Martin Neumeyer reports that in the Los Angeles county there were seventy-two local councils operating to coordinate services in the area.[23]

In World War I, councils had been organized in the heat of international conflict and the government emphasized the need for developing public morale through these councils. In 1940 the organization of councils became centered on developing an efficient defense program. The advisory Commission to the Council of National Defense had distributed memoranda regarding state and local councils even before the war had begun.[24] More than 11,000 local councils became established during the war, some effective, some not. They were set up as separate organizations from those councils already established, and devoted their activities solely to defense.[25] The *Social Work Yearbook* (1945) reported that at the end of the war there were permanent city-wide planning bodies for welfare purposes in approximately 350 cities in the United States. This estimate included all cities over 500,000 and a large proportion of those over 100,000.[26]

Stroup reports that in the summer of 1948, Community Chests and Councils of America conducted a survey to discover the extent of neighborhood councils. Of the fifty cities which received questionnaires, thirteen replied. In these thirteen cities, there were seventy-three neighborhood units of which forty were delegate councils.[27] In 1949, Community Chests and Councils of America published the results of a survey of some 140 Community Welfare Councils. The following summary gives a great deal of insight into the structure and composition of the councils surveyed in cities whose populations range from "less than 50,000" to "1,000,000 and over:"[28]

> Approximately 75 per cent of the organization members of the "average" Council are operating agencies, about one-fourth of which are governmental and the remainder voluntary agencies. . . . All of the Councils except two, both in the less than 50,000 population group, report that governmental agencies are affiliated as members.
>
> Civic and professional organizations are members of 132 of the 139 Councils reporting. However none of the Councils confines membership to operating agencies, since the seven Councils without civic and professional organization members provide for delegates-at-large in addition to those representing member agencies.
>
> Civic and professional organizations represent varying proportions of total Council membership in the different size communities ranging from almost half for the smallest Councils, to less than 10 per cent for Councils in the largest communities. However, the average number of civic and professional organizations affiliated as members shows little variation by size of Council.
>
> The smaller Councils have business, fraternal and veteran's organizations and service and women's clubs as member agencies more commonly than do the larger Councils. There is no apparent relationship between size of Council and membership of improvement associations, religious organizations, unions and professional groups except that professional social work groups participate more frequently in the larger Councils.

Types of Councils in Summary

Many types of councils have developed as part of the community organization movement since the establishment of the first councils of social agencies in Pittsburgh and Milwaukee in 1909. Two basic types may be noted: 1) special interest councils, and 2) general community councils.

Special interest councils would include such diverse associations as welfare councils, health councils, film councils, defense councils, church councils, sectarian councils, youth councils, Girl Scout councils, etc. The community council may be defined as having the following characteristics: 1) local in character, 2) designed to serve the whole community, 3) representative of all major associations (private and public), 4) voluntary in membership and leardership, 5) operating on basis of free democratic discussions and decision-making, 6) having multiple objectives but with the single purpose of improving the quality of life in the community, 7) designed to last over an indefinite period of time.

Modern Approaches

As the size of the community increases, the problems appear more complex and the number of specialized approaches for their treatment also increases. It is a question whether some of these approaches can be included as part of the community organization movement which is now fairly institutionalized. These approaches can be summarized as follows: 1) *Institutionalized* efforts to change attitudes and meet human needs. This would include recreational, educational, and therapeutic methods. Most social problems are amenable to many different types of treatment but seldom are completely solved by means of any single one. For example, the reduction of juvenile delinquency is today approached through Boys Clubs, the Y.M.C.A., Boy Scouts, School Social Workers, Welfare Councils sponsoring street corner workers, etc. Each approach has developed a rationale of its own and is coming to require professional training. 2) *Legal* efforts to work through the law courts and government agencies. These require compulsion to act in a certain way along with voluntary action. Examples would be city planning (a distinct movement in itself), urban renewal, urban conservation commission programs, local efforts of the N.A.A.C.P. 3) *Power* blocks organized to counterbalance or fight power with power. Such approaches may result in court action. However, they are characterized by the intentional organization of economic and political leaders into new formal arrangements which constitute a realignment of the power structure.[29] 4) *Nonviolent* efforts based on moral or ethical principles. This approach may ignore the legal framework, or the professional interests, or the coercive power of upper status individuals in the community, and rally the oppressed groups toward peaceful demonstrations against what they believe to be exploitation or injustices perpetrated by the dominant groups.[30] 5) *Total neighborhood organization* to deal with problems of interest to everyone. This approach focuses upon creating autonomous communities within the larger city. One of the first programs which was able to demonstrate that grass-roots democracy could be created in the unorganized blighted neighborhoods of the metropolis was the Chicago Area Project under the leadership of Clifford Shaw. A more recent example of this approach is the Hyde Park-Kenwood Community Conference.[31]

Community Organization Today

In the 1950's professionals in the field of community organization began sensing they had something in common and that national meetings would be fruitful. Conferences were held informally in different parts of the country to discuss possibilities of organizing nationally. Special sections for people interested in community organization were set aside in the annual meetings of professionals in allied fields such as adult education, social work, university extension work, and functional education. However, no definite national organization ever appeared. Part of the reason for this very likely lies in the fact that the philosophy underlying the community organization movement has not yet comprehended or integrated the diversity and incongruities that have arisen in the modern approaches.

Since its origin in the closely connected movements of the local survey and the local council, the community organization movement has continued to emphasize that kind of social action which is voluntary and seeks to rationally coordinate the organizational activities of a community into effective action programs. As formal approaches to community action, the radical power tactics and radical nonviolent techniques are a challenge to the traditional "cooperative" and "rational" principles in community organization. Power tactics are not always cooperative, and non-

violence is not necessarily rational. At the same time the movement has never fully reconciled its emphasis upon the "voluntary"
nature of community action with the legal coercive practices of
city planning. The fact is that community organization has failed
in many cases to come to grips with some of the most difficult
and entrenched problems of community life and is challenged by
the success of other efforts to deal with community problems.

CITY PLANNING MOVEMENT

The history of city planning has had a parallel development
with those movements which we have just described. At different
historical points the city planning movement could be seen to
overlap with other specific movements interested in treating
community problems. For example, the Pittsburgh survey of 1907
was as much a landmark in the history of city planning as in the
history of community organization. City planning has also become an important part of training (and community consultation)
of institutions of higher education.

The distinctive feature of this movement has been its emphasis
upon physical planning. A statement made following an early
survey (1929) of the scope of city planning at that time, fairly
well summarizes the professional interests today.[32]

> A commonly used classification divides a comprehensive city
> plan into six main elements: zoning, streets, transit, transportation
> (rail, water, and air), public recreation, and civic art or civic
> appearance. Taken together, street planning, land subdivision
> regulations, and zoning are counted on to motive the types of
> land development and housing which the city plan aims to
> secure, so that in many plans housing does not appear as a
> separated element.

City planning has had its own movements (e.g., the city-
beautiful movement) and its own problems (e. g., partial vs.
comprehensive planning). It is presently undergoing a basic
redefinition of its scope and purpose. The extent of this change
and its meaning in the practice of city planning is something for
the future to determine.

Louis Wirth looked toward a mergence of the two movements,

community organization and planning, in a foreword he wrote to a text dealing with this subject. After describing the impetus which World War II gave to community organization, he continues by saying:[33]

> . . the community organization movement gave evidence of converging with another, more recent tendency in American life, namely the increasing recognition of the need for, and possibility of local and regional planning. The planning movement, unlike the community organization movement, represented from its very beginning a close union of governmental and citizen effort, and a corresponding sharing of responsibility by public and private bodies. As local, regional and national planning programs began to enlarge their scope from the initial, virtually exclusive interest in physical development, to an interest in all of the major problems of the common affairs of men living under conditions of interdependence, it became increasingly evident that community organization and planning were two aspects of the same thing. Just as the line demarcating public from private responsibility for the common welfare is constantly shifting and frequently fades out altogether, so the distinction between community organization and planning is gradually being erased. The two movements are rapidly merging into a single integrated set of objectives and techniques.

In Summary

Conditions which were considered undesirable in the religious and economic institutions of Europe led to the Protestant Reformation and Utopian Socialism. Elements in these two movements led to the communitarian movement in the United States which believed that a new way of life could be established. The movement, however, did not grow sufficiently to influence the formation of American community life. Other larger forces were at work, eventually producing conditions which were again found to be undesirable. In an effort to eliminate these conditions in the new world, in the latter half of the nineteenth century welfare reform movements arose which located workers and established agencies in the community. The proliferation of social agencies to treat local problems led to the creation of the community council and the community survey as methods for promoting more efficiency and unity in community work. This was the beginning of what came to be called the community organization movement by social workers who formalized it within their professional field. Within this movement numerous special approaches have developed to treat particular problems in the community. Closely associated with this movement, but having its own history, was the city planning movement. Parallel to both of these movements was the increased attention which institutions of higher education began to give to scientific studies of the community and field work programs.

The field of community action may be in the throes of a new movement which is building from the work of its predecessors. It is growing on the one hand from a realization of the limitations that exist in each of the separate approaches to treating the whole community, and on the other hand from a feeling of the advantage to be derived from combining them into a more integrated and complete effort to create a better way of life at the community level.

THE FUTURE

Increasingly in recent years, the phrase "community development" has been used by consultants to indicate a more comprehensive approach to community action. In overseas programs the phrase has become associated with government-sponsored projects. In the United States it has remained non-political in origin and administration, but it has meant fundamental changes in the physical, social, economic, as well as the political character of the community. The philosophy and the mechanics for managing it as a specific movement are just emerging. The term has come to include city planning, zoning, fact-finding, community organization, and basically all the other problems and major activities discussed in the cases herein. It has begun to circumscribe both the idealism and the reality existing in the efforts of people to improve the quality of life in their local communities. It contains the features of Utopian thought in modern form but with the checks and balances of scientific research. What particular delineations this phase of the community movement will assume in the future remains to be seen.

NOTES

1. The sociological position assumed in this interpretation is Durkheim's that the origins of social processes are sought in prior social processes ("social facts"), not in "states of individual consciousness." (Emile Durkheim, *The Rules of Sociological Method,* Chicago: University of Chicago Press, 1938.)

2. The term "communitarian" was phrased in a book describing the sectarian and Owenite phases of Socialism in America between 1663 and 1829. Arthur E. Bestor, Jr., *Backwoods Utopias* (Philadelphia: University of Pennsylvania Press, 1950).

3. This selection of principles oversimplifies the complexities of these writers, only to stress those common to this movement. A more detailed sketch of the Utopian emphasis as contrasted with the Marxian may be found in Martin Buber, *Paths in Utopia* (Beacon Press, 1949).

4. Henrik F. Infield, *Cooperative Communities at Work* (New York: The Dryden Press, 1945), pp. 13-14.

5. Some of these contemporary settlements have been studied. See Henrik Infield, *The American Intentional Communities,* 1955.

6. Arthur Gallion and Simon Eisner, *The Urban Pattern* (Princeton, N. J.: D. Van Nostrand Co., Inc., 1950) p. 92.

7. Jesse Steiner, *Community Organization* (New York: The Century Co., 1925), pp. 116-17.

8. Robert Park, "Sociology, Community and Society" in *Human Communities* (Glencoe, Illinois: The Free Press, 1952), p. 182.

9. August Hollingshead, "Community Research: Development and Present Condition," *American Sociological Review,* April, 1948, pp. 136-39.

10. The names of early publications were secured by reference to Howard Odum, *American Sociology* (New York: Longmans, Green and Co., 1951), pp. 297-306.

11. Katherine Lackey, *Community Development Through University Extension,* Community Development Publication 3, Southern Illinois University, 1960.

12. William Biddle, *The Cultivation of Community Leaders* (New York: Harper & Brothers, 1953).

13. Severyn Bruyn, "Institutional Approaches" (unpublished manuscript, 1955), pp. 1, 2.

14. Steiner, *op. cit.,* p. 194.

15. Frank Bruno, *Trends in Social Work* (New York: Columbia University Press, 1948), p. 193.

16. *Teamwork in Our Town: Through a Community Welfare Council,* Community Chests and Councils of America, 1950, p. 2.

17. Steiner states that the emergence of community councils was as much a part of rural settings as of urban ones. Steiner, *op. cit.*, p. 162.

18. Kenneth Beam, *Community Coordination*, Vol. VIII, No. 6, November-December, p. 7.

19. Ray Johns and David DeMarche, *Community Organization and Agency Responsibility* (New York: Association Press, 1951), p. 86.

20. As reported in Dillick, *op. cit.*, p. 112.

21. "A Guide to Community Coordination" (Coordinating Councils Inc., 145 W. 12 th St., Los Angeles, California, 1941), p. 2.

22. Howard McClusky "Twelve Years of Community Councils in Michigan," *School of Education Bulletin*, Vol. 20, No. 8, May, 1949, p. 114.

23. Martin Neumeyer, "Coodinating Councils Face Problems of Defense," *Community Coordination*, Vol. VIII, No. 6, November-December, 1940, p. 11.

24. Beam, *op. cit.*, p. 9.

25. Dillick, *op. cit.*, p. 128.

26. Dillick, *op. cit.*, p. 150.

27. Herbert H. Stroup, *Community Welfare Organization*, (New York: Harper & Brothers, 1952), p. 207.

28. *Facts on Council Operations*, Community Chests and Councils of America, Inc., New York 17, N. Y., Bulletin No. 145, June, 1949, p. 3.

29. Saul Alinsky, *Reveille For Radicals* (Chicago: The University of Chicago Press, 1945).

30. Martin Luther King, *Stride Toward Freedom* (New York: Harper & Brothers, 1958).

31. Julia Abrahamson, *A Neighborhood Finds Itself* (New York: Harper & Brothers, 1959).

32. Theodora Kimball Hubbard, and Henry Vincent Hubbard, *Out Cities Today and Tomorrow*, (Cambridge: Harvard University Press, 1929), p. 109 as quoted in Caplow, Theodore, ed., City Planning, *A Selection of Readings in Its Theory and Practice* (Minneapolis: Burgess Publishing Co., 1950), p. 48.

33. Arthur Hillman, *Community Organization and Planning* (New York: The Macmillan Company, 1950), Foreword, pp. xvii-xviii.

BIBLIOGRAPHY

Books

ALINSKY, SAUL. *Reveille for Radicals.* Chicago: University of Chicago Press, 1945.

ARNOLD, WILLIAM R. *Social Movements of Parents in Five Communities For Better Care of Mentally Retarded Children.* M.A. thesis, University of Illinois, 1956.

BLUMER, HERBERT. "Social Movements," in *New Outlines of the Principles of Sociology.* Lee, Alfred, (ed.) New York: Barnes & Nobel Inc, 1946.

BROWNELL, BAKER. *The College and the Community.* New York: Harper & Brothers, 1952.

————. *The Human Community.* New York: Harper & Brothers, 1950.

BRUNO, FRANK. *Trends in Social Work.* New York: Columbia University Press, 1948.

BUBER, MARTIN. *Paths in Utopia.* Boston: Beacon Press, 1949.

CAPLOW, THEODORE, ed. "City Planning," *A Selection of Readings in Its Theory and Practice.* Minneapolis: Burgess Publishing Co.

CORNELL, FRANCES. *The Essentials of Educational Statistics.* New York: John Wiley and Sons Inc., 1956.

DILLICK, SIDNEY. *Community Organization for Neighborhood Development—Past and Present.* Women's Press and Wm. Morrow & Co., 1953.

DURKHEIM, EMILE. *The Rules of Sociological Method.* Chicago: University of Chicago Press, 1938.

FROMM, ERICH. *Escape From Freedom.* New York: Rinehart and and Co., 1941.

GALLION, ARTHUR; EISNER, SIMON. *The Urban Pattern.* Princeton, N. J.: D. Van Nostrand Co., Inc., 1950.

HILLMAN, ARTHUR. *Community Organization and Planning.* New York: The MacMillian Co., 1950.

HUBBARD, THEODORA K.; HUBBARD, HENRY V. *Our Cities Today and Tomorrow.* Cambridge: Harvard University Press, 1929.

HUNTER, FLOYD. *Community Organization, Action and Inaction.* Chapel Hill: University of North Carolina Press, 1953

HUXLEY, ALDOUS. *Brave New World.* New York: Harper Co., 1960.

INFIELD, HENRIK F. *Cooperative Communities at Work.* New York: The Dryden Press, 1945.

JOHNS, RAY; DEMARCHE, DAVID. *Community Organization and Agency Responsibility*. New York: Association Press, 1951.

LIPPITT, RONALD, *et al. The Dynamics of Planned Change*. New York: Harcourt, Brace and Co., 1958.

McIVER, ROBERT M.; PAGE, CHARLES. *Society*. New York: Rinehart & Co., Inc., 1949.

MERTON, ROBERT. *Social Theory and Social Structure*. Glencoe, Illinois: The Free Press, 1949.

MURPHY, CAMPBELL. *Community Organization Practice*. Boston: Houghton Mifflin Co., 1954.

ODUM, HOWARD. *American Sociology*. New York: Longmans, Green and Co., 1951.

ORWELL, GEORGE. *1984*. New York: Harcourt, Brace and Co., 1949.

PARK, ROBERT. *Human Communities*. Glencoe, Illinois: The Free Press, 1952.

POSTON, RICHARD. *Democracy Is You*. New York: Harper & Brothers, 1954.

———. *Small Town Renaissance*. New York: Harper & Brothers, 1950.

POWERS, EDWIN; WITMER, HELEN. *An Experiment in the Prevention of Delinquency*. New York: Columbia University Press, 1951.

REISMAN, DAVID; DENNEY, REUEL; GLAZER, NATHAN. *The Lonely Crowd*. New Haven, Conn.: Yale University Press, 1950.

ROSS, MURRAY G. *Case Histories in Community Organization*. New York: Harper & Brothers, 1958.

SANDERS, IRWIN T. *The Community*. New York: The Ronald Press Co., 1958.

SOWER, CHRISTOPHER; HOLLAND, JOHN; TIEDKE, KENNETH; FREEMAN, WALTER. *Community Involvement*. Glencoe, Illinois: The Free Press, 1957.

STEINER, JESSE. *Community Organization*. New York: The Century Co., 1925.

STROUP, HERBERT. *Social Work*. New York: American Book Co., 1948.

THOMAS, W. I. *The Unadjusted Girl*. Boston: Little, Brown and Co., 1923.

TURNER, RALPH; KILLIAN, LEWIS. *Collective Behavior*. New York: Prentice-Hall, 1957.

WARNER, LLOYD W. *American Life: Dream and Reality*. Chicago: The University of Chicago Press, 1953.

WARNER, LLOYD; MEEKER, MARCHIA; EELLS, KENNETH. *Social Class in America*. Science Research Associates, 1949.

WHYTE, JR., WILLIAM H. *The Organization Man*. New York: Simon and Schuster, 1956.

Pamphlets

A Guide to Community Coordination, Coordinating Councils Inc., 145 W. 12th Street, Los Angeles, California, 1941.

A Report on the Plans and Operations of the Department of Community Development, Southern Illinois University, Carbondale, Illinois, n.d.

BEAM, KENNETH. *Community Coordination*, Volume VIII, November-December, Number 6, 1940.

Change the Street, Chicago Area Project, 907 South Wolcott Avenue, Chicago 12, Illinois, n.d.

Community Planning for Social Welfare, A Policy Statement, Community Chests and Councils of America, Inc., 155 East 44th Street, New York, 1958.

Facts on Council Operations, Community Chests and Councils of America, Inc., New York 17, New York, Bulletin Number 145, June, 1949.

Health and Welfare Planning in the Smaller Community, Community Chests and Councils, Inc., 155 East 44th Street, New York 17, New York, 1945.

Neighbors Unite for Better Communities, Community Chests and Councils of America, Inc., 345 East 46th Street, New York 17, New York, 1956.

Organizing a Community Council, Report of a Committee of the Michigan Council on Adult Education, Bulletin Number 330, published by Superintendent of Public Instruction, 1944.

STONE, WALTER L. *Community Welfare Planning and Organization*, Informal Education Services, Hanover, Indiana, 1949.

Teamwork in Our Town Through a Community Welfare Council, Community Chests and Councils of America, Inc., 155 East 44th Street, New York 17, New York, 1950.

Tool Chest for Community Development Leaders, Pamphlet No. 1, Community Development Institute, Southern Illinois University, n.d.

SUGGESTED READINGS

I. HISTORICAL PERSPECTIVE

How communities have emerged in the past

The Ancient City, Fustel de Coulanges (New York: Doubleday Anchor, 1956; Original: Boston: Lee & Shepard, 1864).

Babylon, Albert Champdor (New York: Putnam, 1958).

Cities in Evolution, Patrick Geddes (London: Williams & Norgate, 1915; New Edition: London: Williams & Norgate, 1949).

The City, Max Weber (Glencoe, Ill.: Free Press, 1958).

The City in History, Lewis Mumford (New York: Harcourt, Brace & World, 1961).

The City of Genoa, Robert W. Carden (London: Pott, 1908).

Daily Life in Ancient Rome, Jerome Carcopino (New Haven: Yale University Press, 1940).

The Making of Dutch Towns: A Study in Urban Development from the Tenth to the Seventeenth Centuries, Gerald L. Burke (London: Cleavor-Hume, 1956).

Medieval Cities: Their Origins and the Revival of Trade, Henri Pirenne (Princeton, N.J.: Princeton University Press, 1925).

The Nature of Cities: Origin, Growth, and Decline, Ludwig Hilberseimer (Chicago: Theobald, 1955).

Pompeii, Roger Carrington (London: Oxford University Press, 1936).

The Preindustrial City: Past and Present, Gideon Sjobert (Glencoe, Ill.: Free Press, 1960).

The Rise of the City: 1878-1898, Arthur Schlesinger (New York: Macmillan, 1933).

Concisely summarized histories of the community may be found in the following:

Urban Behavior, Gordon E. Ericksen (New York: Macmillan, 1954).

The Urban Pattern, Arthur Gallion (Princeton, N.J.: Van Nostrand, 1958).

Urban Society, William Cole (Cambridge, Mass.: Riverside Press, 1958).

Urban Society, Noel P. Gist and L. A. Halbert (New York: Thomas Y. Crowell, 1956).

Urban Sociology, Ernest Bergel (New York: McGraw-Hill, 1955).

II. THE PHILOSOPHICAL PERSPECTIVE

The larger meaning of community and its moral or ethical importance to man

A. SOCIAL PHILOSOPHY

Between Man and Man, Martin Buber (Boston: Beacon Press, 1947).

Community Welfare Organization, "The Ideal Community," Herbert Stroup (New York: Harper, 1952).

The Culture of Cities, Lewis Mumford (New York: Harcourt, Brace & Co., 1938).

The Human Community, Baker Brownell (New York: Harper, 1950).

The Quest for Community, Robert A. Nisbet (New York: Oxford University Press, 1953).

Rebuilding Rural America, "The Ruralist Philosophy," Earl Hitch (New York: Harper, 1950).

The Republic, Plato, trans. F. M. Cornford (New York: Oxford University Press, 1945).

Solitude and Society, Nicholas Berdyaev (London: Centenary Press, 1949).

The Writings of Martin Buber, Will Herberg, ed. (New York: Meridian Books, 1956).

B. UTOPIAS AND SOCIAL CRITICISM

1. *Modern Analyses*

The End of Ideology, Daniel Bell (Glencoe, Ill.: Free Press, 1960).

The Sane Society, Erich Fromm (New York: Rinehart, 1959).

2. *Utopias*

Backwoods Utopias, The Sectarian and Owenite Phases of Communitarian Socialism in America: 1663-1829, Arthur Bestor, Jr. (Philadelphia: University of Pennsylvania Press, 1950).

The Story of Utopias, Lewis Mumford (New York: Viking, 1962).

3. *Cooperatives*

All Things Common, Claire Bishop (New York: Harper, 1950).

Masters of Their Own Destiny, M. M. Coady (New York: Harper, 1939).

Cooperative Group Living, Henrik F. Infield and Joseph B. Maier, eds. (New York: Henry Koosis & Co., 1950).

C. FICTIONAL WORKS

1. *Classics*

Erewhon and Erewhon Revisited, Samuel Butler (New York: Modern Library, 1933).

Ideal Commonwealths, Henry Morley, ed. (New York: Cooperative Publications Society, 1901).

Looking Backward, Edward Bellamy (New York: Modern Library, 1951).

2. *Modern Novels*

Babbitt, Sinclair Lewis (New York: Grosset & Dunlap, 1922).

Cry, the Beloved Country, Alan Paton (New York: Scribner's Sons, 1948).

The Hamlet, William Faulkner (New York: Random House, 1940).

To Kill a Mockingbird, Harper Lee (Philadelphia: Lippincott, 1960).

Main Street, Sinclair Lewis (New York: Harcourt, Brace, 1921).

The Mansion, William Faulkner (New York: Random House, 1940).

The Town, William Faulkner (New York: Random House, 1957).

3. *Modern Satire*

Brave New World, Aldous Huxley (New York: Harper, 1960).

1984, George Orwell (New York: Harcourt, Brace, 1949).

III. THE SOCIOLOGICAL PERSPECTIVE

Approaches to the study of community within the sociological tradition

A. THE CONCEPT OF COMMUNITY

Approaches to Community Development, Phillips Ruopp, ed. (The Hague: W. Van Hoeve, 1953).

Community, Robert MacIver (New York: Macmillan, 1924).

"The Community As a Social Group," E. T. Hiller, *American Sociological Review,* VI (1941), 189-202.

Community Life and Social Policy, Louis Wirth (Chicago: University of Chicago Press, 1956).

"Definition of the City," Robert Maurier, *American Journal of Sociology,* XV (1910), 536-48.

"Definitions of Community," George Hillery, Jr., *Rural Sociology*, XX (1955), 111-23.

Human Communities, Robert Park (Glencoe, Ill.: Free Press, 1952).

An Introduction of Social Science, Don Calhoun, *et al.*, eds., "The Nature of the Community" (Philadelphia: Lippincott, 1953), pp. 3-24.

The Little Community, Robert Redfield (Chicago: University of Chicago Press, 1955).

The Political Community: A Study of Anomie, Sebastian De Grazia (Chicago: University of Chicago Press, 1948).

"Toward an Interactional Conception of Community" Harold Kaufman, *Social Forces*, XXXVIII (1959), pp. 8-17.

B. Typologies

Ideal or constructed typologies used in analyzing community

Community and Society, Ferdinand Tonnies (E. Lansing, Mich.: University of Michigan Press, 1957).

The Division of Labor in Society, Émile Durkheim (Glencoe, Ill.: Free Press, 1949).

"Folk-Society," Robert Redfield, *American Journal of Sociology*, LII (1947), 293-308.

Modern Sociological Theory, Howard Becker (ed.), "Methodology, Procedures, and Techniques in Sociology," John McKinney, pp. 224-28; and "Current Sacred-Secular Theory and its Development," Howard Becker, pp. 133-85 (New York: Dryden Press, 1957).

Village Communities in the East and West, Sir Henry Maine (New York: Holt, 1889).

C. Methods for Studying the Community

"Community Research: Development and Present Condition," *American Sociological Review*, XIII (1948), 136-46.

"The Community-Study Method," *The American Journal of Sociology*, Conrad M. Arensberg, LX (1954), 109-24.

The Little Community, Robert Redfield (Chicago: University of Chicago Press, 1955).

"The Participant Observer Technique in Small Communities," Florence Kluckhohn, *American Journal of Sociology*, XLVI (1940), 331-43.

Preparing a Community Profile: The Methodology of a Social Reconnaisance (Lexington, Ky.: Bureau of Community Service, 1952).

"The Role of the Researcher as Participant Observer and Participant-as-Observer in the Field Situation," Nicholas Babchuk, *Human Organization,* XXI (1962), 225.

Scientific Social Surveys and Research, Pauline Young (Englewood Cliffs, N.J.: Prentice-Hall, 1956).

"Some Logical and Methodological Problems in Community Research," Albert J. Reiss, *Social Forces,* XXXIII (1954), 51-64.

"The Study of Culture: A Survey of Technique and Methodology in Field Work," John W. Bennett, *American Sociological Review,* XIII (1948), 672-89.

D. THE ECOLOGICAL PERSPECTIVE

1. *Human Communities*

The City, Park, Burgess, and McKenzie, "The Growth of the City," Ernest Burgess (Chicago, Ill.: University of Chicago Press, 1925).

Human Ecology, Amos Hawley (New York: Ronald Press, 1950).

Human Ecology, James Quinn (New York: Prentice-Hall, 1950).

"The Nature of Cities," C. O. Harris and L. Ullman, *The Annals of the American Academy of Political and Social Science,* CCXLVII (1945), 7-17.

"Sentiment and Symbolism as Ecological Variables," Walter Firey, *American Sociological Review,* X (1945), 140-48.

2. *Plant and Animal Communities*

Cells and Societies, John Bonner (Princeton, N.J.: Princeton University Press, 1955).

Elements of Ecology, George Clark (New York: John Wiley, 1954).

The Social Insects and Their Origin and Evolution, William Wheeler (New York: Harcourt, Brace, 1928).

The Study of Plant Communities, Henry J. Oosting (San Francisco: W. H. Freeman, 1956).

E. THE DEMOGRAPHIC PERSPECTIVE

Population Problems, Warren Thompson (New York: McGraw-Hill, 1953).

Social Characteristics of Urban and Rural Communities, Otis Duncan and Albert Reiss (New York: U.S. Census Monograph Series, 1956).

The Structure of the Metropolis Community: A Study of Dominance and Subdominance, Don J. Bogue (E. Lansing, Mich.: University of Michigan Press, 1949).

The Urban South, Rupert Vance and Nicholas J. Demerath (Chapel Hill, N.C.: University of North Carolina Press, 1954).

F. OTHER SOCIOLOGICAL PERSPECTIVES

The American Community, Blaine Mercer, Part Two: "The Community Culture" (New York: Random House, 1956), pp. 53-89.

American Community Behavior, Ch. 4: "Social Order and Institutions," Jessie Bernard (New York: Holt, Rinehart and Winston, 1962), pp. 42-59.

American Life: Dream and Reality, W. Lloyd Warner (Chicago: University of Chicago Press, 1953).

The Eclipse of Community, Maurice R. Stein (Princeton, N.J.: Princeton University Press, 1960).

The Human Group, George Homans (New York: Harcourt, Brace, 1950).

G. COMMUNITY STUDIES

Black Metropolis, St. Clair Drake and Horace Cayton (New York: Harcourt, Brace, 1945).

Caste and Class in a Southern Town, John Dollard (New Haven: Yale University Press, 1937).

Community Power Structure, Floyd Hunter (Chapel Hill, N. C.: University of North Carolina Press, 1952).

Crestwood Heights: A Study of the Culture of Suburban Life, John R. Seely, R. Alexander Sim, and Elizabeth W. Loosely (New York: Basic Books, Inc., 1956).

Deep South, Allison Davis and Burleigh Gardner (Chicago: University of Chicago Press, 1941).

Democracy in Jonesville, W. Lloyd Warner and Associates (New York: Harper, 1949).

Elmtown's Youth, August Hollingshead (New York: John Wiley, 1949).

Family and Community Life in Ireland, Conrad Arensberg and Solon T. Kimball (Cambridge, Mass.: Harvard University Press, 1959).

The Gold Coast and the Slum, Henry Zorbaugh (Chicago: University of Chicago Press, 1929).

The Governing of Men, Alexander Leighton (Princeton, N.J.: Princeton University Press, 1945).

Greenwich Village, Caroline Ware (Boston: Houghton Mifflin, 1955).

Life in a Mexican Village: Tepoztlán Revisited, Oscar Lewis (Urbana, Ill.: University of Illinois Press, 1951).

Middletown, Robert and Helen Lynd (New York: Harcourt, Brace, 1929).

Middletown in Transition, Robert and Helen Lynd (New York: Harcourt, Brace, 1937).

Plainville, U.S.A., James West (New York: Columbia University Press, 1945).

Small Town in Mass Society, Arthur J. Vidich and Joseph Bensman (Princeton, N.J.: Princeton University Press, 1958).

Social History of a War-Boom Community, Robert Havighurst and H. G. Morgan (Toronto, Canada: Longmans, 1951).

The Social Life of a Modern Community, W. Lloyd Warner and Paul S. Lunt (New Haven, Conn.: Yale University Press, 1941).

Street Corner Society, William Foote Whyte (Chicago: University of Chicago Press, 1955).

Tenants of the Almighty, Arthur F. Raper (New York: Macmillan, 1943).

We Americans, Elin E. Anderson (Cambridge, Mass.: Harvard University Press, 1937).

H. The Metropolitan Region

The Death and Life of Great American Cities, Jane Jacobs (New York: Random House, 1961).

Governing of the Metropolis, Scott Greer (New York: John Wiley, 1962).

The Image of the City, Kevin Lynch (Cambridge: Cambridge Technology Press, 1960).

Megalopolis, Jean Gottman (New York: Twentieth Century Fund, 1961).

A Natural History of New York City, John Keiram (Boston: Houghton Mifflin, 1959).

The Suburban Community, William Dobriner (New York: Putnam, 1958).

Suburbia, Robert Wood (Boston: Houghton Mifflin, 1959).

IV. THE STUDY OF COMMUNITY ACTION

Approaches to the study of communities in action

A. CONCEPTS: THE MEANING OF THE TERMS "COMMUNITY DEVELOPMENT" AND "COMMUNITY ORGANIZATION"

Community: An Introduction to a Social System, Irwin T. Sanders, Ch. 20: "Community Development" (New York: Ronald Press, 1958), pp. 389-410.

Community Organization: Theory and Practice, Murray Ross (New York: Harper, 1955).

Community Organization Practice, Campbell Murphy (Boston: Houghton Mifflin, 1954).

Community Structure and Analysis, Marvin Sussman (ed.), Ch. 5: "The Developmental Concept," William Biddle (New York: Thomas Y. Crowell, 1959), pp. 115-28.

Community Structure and Change, Lowry Nelson, Charles Ramsey, Coolie Vernor, Ch. 20: "Community Development" (New York: Macmillan, 1960).

B. COMMUNITY ACTION PROGRAMS: CASE STUDIES

Building a Better Home Town, H. Clay Tate (New York: Harper, 1954).

Case Histories in Community Organization, Murray Ross (New York: Harper, 1958).

Community Involvement, Christopher Sower, John Holland, Kenneth Tiedke, Walter Freeman (Glencoe, Ill.: Free Press, 1937).

Community Organization: Action and Inaction, Floyd Hunter, Ruth Shaffer, Cecil Sheps (Chapel Hill, N.C.: University of North Carolina Press, 1956).

Dynamics of Group at Work, Herbert Thelen (Chicago: University of Chicago Press, 1954).

The Health of Regionville: What People Thought and Did About It, Earl Lomon Koos (New York: Columbia University Press, 1949).

Kentucky on the March, Harry Schacter (New York: Harper, 1949).

A Neighborhood Finds Itself, Julia Abrahamson (New York: Harper, 1959).

The People Act: Stories of How Americans Are Coming Together to Deal with Their Community Problems, E. M. McFee (New York: Harper, 1955).

Rebuilding Rural America, Earl Hitch (New York: Harper, 1950).

Small Communities in Action: Stories of Citizen Programs at Work, Jean and Jess Ogden (New York: Harper, 1946).

Small Town Renaissance, Richard W. Poston (New York: Harper, 1950).

The Talladega Story: A Study in Community Process, Solon T. Kimball and Marion Pearsall (University, Ala.: University of Alabama Press, 1954).

TVA and the Grass Roots: A Study in the Sociology of Formal Organization, Philip Selznick (Berkeley, Calif.: University of California Press, 1949).

C. Special Planning Fields

1. Small Community Planning

Democracy Is You, Richard W. Poston (New York: Harper, 1954).

Exploring the Small Community, Otto Hoiberg (Lincoln, Neb.: University of Nebraska Press, 1955).

Making Good Communities Better, Irwin T. Sanders (Lexington, Ky.: University of Kentucky Press, 1952).

The Small Community Looks Ahead, Wayland J. Hayes (New York: Harcourt, Brace, 1949).

Studying Your Community, Roland Warren (New York: Russell Sage Foundation, 1955).

2. City Planning

City and Country in America, David R. Weimer, ed. (New York: Appleton-Century-Crofts, 1962).

Communities: Means of Livelihood and Ways of Life, Percival and Paul Goodman (New York: Vintage Press, 1960).

Exploding Metropolis, by the editors of *Fortune* (New York: Doubleday, 1958).

The Living City, Frank Lloyd Wright (New York: Horizon Press, 1958).

Towards New Towns in America, Clarence Stein (Liverpool: University Press of Liverpool, 1951).

Urban Land Use Planning, F. Stuart Chapin (New York: Harper, 1957).

The Urban Pattern: City Planning and Designing, Arthur Gallion, with Simon Eisner (Princeton, N.J.: Van Nostrand, 1950).

D. International Approaches

Communities and Their Development, T. R. Batten (Fairlawn, N.J.: Oxford University Press, 1957).

Cultural Patterns and Technical Change, Margaret Mead, ed. (Paris: UNESCO, 1957).

Hands Across Frontiers: Case Studies in Technical Cooperation, Howard Teaf, Jr., and Peter Franck (Ithaca, N.Y.: Cornell University Press, 1955).

Human Problems in Technological Change, Edward H. Spicer, ed. (New York: Russell Sage Foundation, 1952).

India's Changing Villages, S. C. Duke (London: Routledge and Kegan Paul, 1958).

Rural Reconstruction in Action: Experience in the Near and Middle East, H. B. Allen (Ithaca, N.Y.: Cornell University Press, 1953).

Technical Cooperation in Latin-American Agriculture, Arthur Mosher (Chicago: University of Chicago Press, 1957).

Toward Freedom from Want from India to Mexico, D. S. Hatch (Fairlawn, N.J.: Oxford University Press, 1949).

Index

INDEX